GUNBOATS
ON THE GREAT
LAKES 1866-68

GUNBOATS
ON THE GREAT
LAKES 1866-68

The British Navy's show of force
at the time of Confederation

Cheryl MacDonald

James Lorimer and Company Ltd., Publishers
Toronto

James Lorimer & Company Ltd., Publishers acknowledges the support of the Ontario
Arts Council (OAC), an agency of the Government of Ontario, which in 2015-16 funded
1,676 individual artists and 1,125 organizations in 209 communities across Ontario for
a total of $50.5 million. We acknowledge the support of the Canada Council for the
Arts, which last year invested $153 million to bring the arts to Canadians throughout the
country. This project has been made possible in part by the Government of Canada and
with the support of the Ontario Media Development Corporation.

 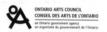

...blication has been supported in part by the Dunnville District Heritage Association.

Cover design: Tyler Cleroux
Cover and interior images courtesy of Toronto Public Library

Library and Archives Canada Cataloguing in Publication

MacDonald, Cheryl, 1952-2016, author
    Gunboats on the Great Lakes, 1866-68 : the British Navy's show of force
at the time of confederation / Cheryl MacDonald.

Includes bibliographical references and index.
Issued in print and electronic formats.
ISBN 978-1-4594-1122-7 (softcover).--ISBN 978-1-4594-1123-4 (EPUB)

    1. Canada--History--Fenian Invasions, 1866-1870. 2. Great Britain.
Navy--History--19th century. 3. Gunboats--History--19th century. 4. Great
Lakes Region (North America)--History, Military--19th century. 5. Canada--
History--19th century. I. Title.

FC480.F4M237 2017   971.04'8   C2017-903193-7
                                                         C2017-903194-5

James Lorimer & Company Ltd., Publishers
117 Peter Street, Suite 304
Toronto, ON, Canada
M5V 0M3
www.lorimer.ca

Printed and bound in Canada.

CONTENTS

*This book is dedicated to the many people who touched
Cheryl MacDonald's life, inspired her, and assisted her in her
decades-long mission to document, recall, and retell the history of
Haldimand and Norfolk Counties, and the
greater Niagara Region.
It is dedicated to museum staff, researchers, local historians
both professional and amateur, friends, families, community
leaders — all of those who assisted her in researching
her multiple books and articles.
To her friends in the re-enactment community who shared her
joy and passion for visually recounting history.
To the people young and old who came from far and wide to
listen to her talks, enjoy her historical tableaux, and share their
stories with her.
Her vast community supported her, encouraged her, and
greatly contributed to the full and rich life she enjoyed and shared
with her loved ones.*

PREFACE

During her thirty-year career, Cheryl MacDonald wrote more than forty books and hundreds of newspaper and magazine articles related to the local history of Haldimand County, Ontario. Her rare gift of making history accessible to everyone made her a much-sought-after speaker as well. In 2012, she received the Queen's Diamond Jubilee Medal in recognition of her work researching and promoting Canadian local history. Cheryl passed away in October 2016 in the midst of finishing the manuscript for this book.

In the early 1990s, Cheryl collaborated with the Dunnville District Heritage Association (DDHA) to produce *Grand Heritage* — the definitive history of the Dunnville, Ontario, area. During this work, she became aware of the intriguing story of the Royal Navy Gunboat *Britomart*. The *Britomart* spent more than two years in rural Haldimand County, most of her time on Lake Erie at Dunnville, in the aftermath of the invasion of Canada by the Fenians in 1866. Cheryl spent the next fifteen years researching the Royal Navy Gunboats that were dispatched to guard the Great Lakes and thwart further Fenian incursions. This almost-forgotten period in Canadian history coincides with a crucial period in the formation of the Confederation.

Before her passing, Cheryl asked that her sister and research assistant, Sandra MacDonald, finish the manuscript and that

DDHA provide funding for publication. Donations from individuals and the York Historical Society supplemented the DDHA contribution.

The final product does not reflect all of the material Cheryl had planned to include. However, *Gunboats on the Great Lakes 1866-68* is especially important as it includes never-before-published information and photographs. Cheryl's highly readable style enhances accessibility to the content and brings the story to life. As such, it is a substantial contribution to the body of knowledge related to the *Britomart*, the *Cherub*, and the *Heron*, the three gunboats that patrolled the Great Lakes around the Ontario towns of Dunnville, Goderich, Hamilton, Kingston, Port Dover, Prescott, St. Catharines, Toronto and Windsor.

April Cormaci

Dunnville District Heritage Association

May 2017

PROLOGUE
Welcome Guests

On November 15, 1866, the citizens of Dunnville, Canada West, pulled out all the stops to pay tribute to the crew of Her Majesty's Gunboat *Britomart*. After arriving late in the summer, the British gunboat had been stationed at the small town on the Grand River, from which the Feeder Canal ran eastward to the strategically important Welland Canal. Just downstream, on Lake Erie, was Port Maitland, which also contributed to Dunnville's prosperity. In 1866, six years after its incorporation as a village, the community fifty-four kilometres southwest of Hamilton had a population of 1,300, making it the largest municipality in Haldimand County. For years, grain, lumber and other goods from the interior had made their way to Dunnville, first by water, and, after the Buffalo, Brantford & Goderich Railway arrived in 1854, by train. By 1866, Dunnville had a number of thriving businesses, many of them housed in buildings of brick or stone, and culture was keeping up with commercial interests. Both a library and weekly newspaper had started more than a decade earlier, and a high school would open by 1868.

One of the most successful operations in Dunnville was Price's Hotel, later known as Price's Farmer's Hotel, located on the site of one of the earliest taverns in the community. Conveniently situated next to both the feeder canal and the open space where the local farmers' market eventually was held, the inn had been purchased by David Price around 1850. A stonemason by trade, Price replaced the wooden structure with a stone building and set about making his hotel one of the most popular destinations in the region. In the process, he turned it into a multi-generational operation that became a local institution. A retrospective of his career written in 1904 noted, "No more painstaking genial landlord is to be found anywhere."[1]

Price certainly made an effort to put on a first-class reception in honour of the *Britomart* crew. The newly completed dining hall was decked with international flags, including the Union Jack, British ensign, and the flags of Norway, Spain, Holland, Brazil, Portugal and the United States, all of them borrowed from the *Britomart*. Despite cold, wet weather, about 150 people — all of them men — had come out for the celebration. There were prominent professionals and businessmen, a smattering of local politicians and members of the Dunnville Naval Brigade, including their leader, the entrepreneur and politician Lachlan McCallum. Unlike the crew of the *Britomart*, the brigade had actually engaged Fenian invaders almost six months earlier when the *W.T. Robb*, one of McCallum's tugs, had been pressed into service as a makeshift gunboat in the early hours of the June invasion.

The festivities started out in the ballroom at 7 p.m., where W.A. MacRae, chairman of the "committee of arrangements," welcomed the sailors with "a very neat and appropriate speech." The evening included singing and several toasts, starting with one to the Queen, then continuing with the Prince and Princess of Wales and the rest of the royal family; the Governor-General; the army, navy and volunteers; and several other noteworthy groups.

Arthur Hildebrand Alington, the gunboat's commander, was expected to respond to some of these. In his neat uniform and imposing side-whiskers, the young lieutenant seemed a fine example of the heroic seamen who had become beloved icons throughout the British Empire. And he was a natural for the role, having grown up among the landed gentry of Lincolnshire where the concepts of duty and leadership were drilled home until they became second nature. It probably did not take Alington much conscious effort to phrase his gracious response to the toasts proffered to him and his men, which Thomas Messenger, publisher of the *Grand River Sachem* newspaper in nearby Caledonia, captured for posterity. At one point, he noted, Lieutenant Alington

> responded in an eloquent and feeling manner, assuring the gentlemen who had just spoken, that himself, his officers and the crew duly appreciated the compliment paid them, and could well understand that it was not given to them personally, but as the representatives of the Navy of Great Britain, which always had, and he felt convinced always would do its duty, whether it were in defending the honor of the flag at home, in any part of Her Majesty's wide dominions, or other parts of the world.[2]

Later on, in response to another toast, he continued in a similar vein:

> He said he looked upon it as a great honor to belong to the British Navy, as it was always ready in case of emergency to uphold the honor of "the flag that had braved a thousand years the battle and the breeze" and he felt that every man on the *Britomart* were [*sic*] of the right stamp — most of them having already seen service, and shown pluck. He was proud of the reception himself, officers and men were now receiving as the representatives of a class, at the hands of the people of Dunnville, and he could assure them that their kindnesses would long be remembered by all who had the honor of participating in it.[3]

Alington struck all the right chords: patriotism, imperial ties, Britain's commitment to defending the colonies and gratitude for the warm hospitality extended to the officers and the crew, not as individuals, but as symbols of the navy upon which British imperial power rested. Some cynics may have scoffed, but most of those in attendance probably were touched by the sentiments expressed, aided no doubt by the amount of liquor consumed. After years of worrying about Fenian attacks, culminating with three invasions between mid-April and early June and the continuing threat of more, Alington's words were precisely what the people of Dunnville and other Canadians needed to hear. They were reassured, confident that they would be protected against the looming dangers, certain that the *Britomart* and her crew had the best interests of the people at Dunnville and the surrounding area at heart.

What may not have been apparent to many in the room was that Alington, or one of his fellow gunboat commanders, might have delivered that same speech anywhere in Canada or the British Empire with very few changes. That November night in Price's Hotel, gunboat diplomacy was very much at work. Its impact would be felt not only by the residents of Dunnville and Haldimand County, but by thousands of Canadians caught up in the anxiety of the times, and ultimately, it would influence the fate of the country.

***

I first learned about the *Britomart* while editing *Grand Heritage* for the Dunnville District Heritage Association. When that history of Dunnville and area was published in 1992, it included about a page of material on the *Britomart*, mostly because that was all we were able to uncover then. But the gunboat had captured my imagination; I was intrigued by the idea that a British gunboat had spent more than two years in rural Haldimand County, on a mission that history books seemed to have forgotten entirely. The story became even more fascinating when I learned that the *Britomart* was just one of the gunboats serving on the Great Lakes around the time of the Fenian invasions, another chapter of Canadian history that does not receive the attention or respect it deserves. Gradually, as I collected material on the *Britomart* and her sister ships, what emerged was a tale that emphasized the importance of diplomacy and public relations in the crucial period when the first four Canadian colonies formed the federation known as the Dominion of Canada. It also became clear how profoundly Canadians were affected by the Fenians, not only as a result of the actual invasions but also because of the tension created by the threat of invasion, both before and after 1866. It is a story that deserves to be told, not just to give readers a better understanding of the impact of the Fenians but also to provide insight into the Canadian psyche at a crucial time in our collective history.

CHAPTER 1
The Fenian Threat

One hundred and fifty years after the first invasions, it is difficult to imagine how the people living in what is now Ontario perceived the Fenians. If 21st-century Canadians consider the Fenian raids at all, it's more likely as a minor incident with comic overtones, carried out by inept, intoxicated invaders who more closely resembled barroom brawlers than battle-hardened soldiers. Generally, though, these invaders are not given much thought, and there are many who do not connect the incidents with Irish-Canadian history. When it comes to that topic, it is the Irish famine that tends to dominate our collective memory with images of "coffin ships" and the horrors of quarantine stations such as Grosse Île. Relatively few Canadians are likely to connect Ireland's centuries-long struggle for freedom from British rule with the events that played out in Canada. Furthermore, most Canadians likely do not realize how strong anti-Irish sentiment was in 19th-century Canada, or how deeply it affected the daily lives of thousands of people. Yet it is not an exaggeration to say, for many Canadians in the 1860s and early 1870s, the Fenians had a reputation that was dramatically similar to that of Muslim terrorists in post-9/11 North America. Racially and religiously different, and consequently deemed inferior, they were looked on as uncultured, barbaric and bent on the violent destruction of 19th-century British society.

The Irish Republican Brotherhood was founded on St. Patrick's Day — March 17 — in 1857 by James Stephens in Ireland. The organization was not much different from the Fenian Brotherhood, founded by John O'Mahony in the United States, and the two soon became indistinguishable. Stephens and O'Mahony had been connected before, and both were passionate supporters of Irish independence. Born in 1816, O'Mahony was the son and nephew of men who had fought in the Irish Rebellion of 1798. Scholarly and serious, he taught Greek and Latin, had studied Sanskrit and also earned reputation as a Gaelic scholar. Although he never completed his degree, he did attend Trinity College and wrote extensively on both political and historical topics. But O'Mahony had a tendency to overextend himself and, on at least one occasion, was confined to a mental institution because of work-related strain. James Stephens, who was eight years younger, was also a dedicated scholar. Although he did not have the same advantages as O'Mahony, he did read extensively. Initially reluctant to be involved in politics, Stephens eventually joined the republican cause. Both he and O'Mahony were involved in the Young Ireland movement, which staged an unsuccessful rebellion in Ireland in 1848.

As the rebellion collapsed, Stephens and O'Mahony fled the country, along with another prominent colleague, Thomas D'Arcy McGee. Stephens returned to Ireland in 1856 and founded the Irish Republic Brotherhood a year later. He then joined O'Mahony in the United States, where O'Mahony had founded a new movement. Members of both were soon known as "the Fenians," after a legendary band of Irish warriors, the *Fianna*.

The Fenians' initial goal in North America was to raise funds to finance action in Ireland, a sensible strategy at a time when first- and second-generation Irish immigrants made up a large percentage of the population. In New York and Boston, about one of every six people had Irish background. In Montreal, approximately a quarter of the population claimed Irish ancestry, and in Canada West, which would soon become Ontario, approximately one in three urban residents was Irish. These numbers gave the Irish considerable political clout, in spite of the rampant prejudice they experienced. Thanks to this, the Fenians had much more freedom to operate in the United States than in Ireland, where their activities were unarguably treasonous. The situation was somewhat different in the Canadian provinces, however, as the territories were still British colonies. Canadian Fenians had to be more secretive, but their connections to the thriving American branch, just a short distance away across a mostly unguarded border, helped the organization grow.

Not that all Irish-Canadians or Irish-Americans were Fenians. Thomas D'Arcy McGee certainly was not, at least not by the time he arrived in Canada. As a teenager, he had emigrated to Boston with a sister because of conflicts with their stepmother. A promising career as a journalist and public speaker earned McGee an invitation back to Ireland, which in turn led to his involvement with Young Ireland. After the 1848 uprising, he fled back to the United States and, for a time, continued to speak and write in favour of Irish liberation, by whatever means necessary. Eventually, however, he became disenchanted with the way the Irish were treated in the United States. He also came to the conclusion the Irish would do best under British rule and Canada offered opportunities that existed nowhere else. Around the time that O'Mahony brought the Fenian organization to the United States, McGee relocated to Montreal and entered politics.

McGee was in many ways typical of the Irish immigrants who chose not to get involved with the Fenians. They tended to be older, more middle class and better educated. The Fenians, with their colourful rhetoric and call for armed rebellion, appealed to younger members of the working class. Not that the general public acknowledged such differences: When Buffalo, New York, held a procession in tribute to assassinated President Abraham Lincoln in April 1865, a Hamilton newspaper correspondent labelled the Irish contingent as Fenians, making no distinction whatsoever between the militant Irish Republican Brotherhood and more moderate Irish immigrants. Similarly, in January 1866, a New York City correspondent reported a "noisy Fenian" on a street car and made no effort to distinguish the culprit from any other Irish immigrant. Several ladies were forced to listen to "the cursing and ribaldry of one of the specimen Brotherhood, who should have been ejected from [the] car, for decency sake, if for nothing else."[1]

Aside from the possibility of an Irish accent, there are no clues as to how the correspondent concluded the man was a Fenian. Perhaps he was relying on earlier newspaper reports, such as a November 1865 item describing a visit by English detectives to Fenian headquarters in New York City:

> Round the door lounged several expensively dressed
> but exceedingly disreputable looking persons —
> their principal characteristics being, slouched hats,
> shaven cheeks and villainous expressions. This
> latter attribute, together with the strong smell of
> over-proof whiskey, declared them to be Fenians.

They also had Irish accents and were able to "swear artistically."[2]

Perhaps accents and obscenities were what alerted a prominent Canadian woman to the presence of Fenians on another occasion. The wife of Canada's governor-general, Lady Elizabeth Monck, was aboard a ship carrying a number of British troops when she wrote, "They seem to me such an ill looking set, I feel sure that we are bringing many Fenians to Canada."[3] Lady Monck was one of many who feared the Fenians had successfully infiltrated the armed forces. As early as 1864, there were reports that the Fenians were trying to recruit soldiers and had planted members in the Montreal militia. There were occasional arrests, including one in Quebec City in October 1865 when two men named O'Brien and Sullivan were taken into custody by a sergeant of the 7th Fusiliers for "endeavoring to seduce soldiers to join the Fenians."[4]

Just before the Fenians invaded Canada West in June 1866, the *New York World* carried a story claiming there were numerous sympathizers in the British army, at least half of whom would join the cause when the Fenians gave the word. That report seemed to be substantiated by a later incident in Montreal in June 1866, as the Prince of Wales Rifles prepared to head for the border to repel an anticipated invasion. As they were about to board the train, a Sergeant-Major Mahony began shouting pro-Fenian slogans and then ran off, pursued by some of his brothers-in-arms. He was soon captured, but not before his actions reinforced the idea that even the soldiers assigned to guard Canadian territory were not above suspicion.[5]

Huge numbers of people came to the illogical conclusion that all Irish were Fenians, and all Fenians terrorists. By the mid-1860s, it was impossible to avoid reports about Fenian activities and the threats they posed to peaceful Victorian society. And, with the Irish seemingly everywhere, it was not surprising that many Canadians truly believed they were continually under threat of attack.

But were they? When John O'Mahony established the Fenian Brotherhood in North America, its main purpose was to raise funds for the cause in Ireland. There was no real plan to attack Canada, although Fenians were encouraged to enlist during the American Civil War, partly because the military training they received would be valuable in the fight for Irish freedom, and partly because they would receive a regular income, some of which could be donated to the cause. As the war drew to a close, Fenian leaders became increasingly aware that it would be advantageous to mobilize these experienced soldiers for the Irish cause. There was also the realization that American authorities might be more likely to support an attack on Canada — or at least look the other way — once the Civil War ended. Although there had been a number of diplomatic crises that inflamed hostile feelings towards Britain and her North American colonies during the war, Lincoln and his government realized all too well that they could not fight the Confederacy *and* the British Empire simultaneously. But once a Northern victory seemed assured, the Fenians could consider an invasion of Canada. At worst, a successful attack might allow them to use Canadian territory as a bargaining chip in negotiations for Irish freedom. At best, the United States could be drawn into the conflict and take over Canadian territory, striking a serious blow against the British Empire.

Initially, the Fenians were divided about their course of action, with some preferring to stick to the organization's original mandate of supporting efforts in Ireland. But, as dissension in the ranks grew, it became increasingly apparent that some kind of military campaign was required. Various possibilities were discussed. Some were practical, others ludicrous, but many details reached the public, usually through newspapers. The press was hungry for stories and in the mid-19th century, just as today, violence and sensationalism sold papers. With very little in the way of checks and balances against libel or inaccurate reporting in place, most newspapers had few qualms about publishing compelling stories before verifying all the facts. The Fenians themselves frequently discussed their plans and strategies in the open, often exaggerating their membership numbers and their financial and military resources for propaganda purposes. Although both British and Canadian spy networks were in place, the information they gathered was frequently inaccurate. Sorting out truth from fiction was next to impossible. Thousands of Canadians were left wondering just how dangerous the Fenians were, with no choice but to depend on rumour and their own anxieties for the answer.

Among the most anxious residents of Canada were members of the Orange Order, a fraternal organization established in Ireland in 1795 to commemorate the Protestant victory of William of Orange (later King William III) at the Battle of the Boyne in 1690. At worst extremely conservative and rabidly anti-Catholic, the Orange Order grew rapidly between 1845 and 1860, especially in Canada West, even though its activities had brought it into disrepute in Britain, where legislated reforms were abolishing discrimination against Catholics. The Order's parades frequently sparked sectarian violence, and by 1850, they were banned in Britain. A decade later, legislation was in the works to keep Orange flags and other symbols out of public view. The organization had fallen into such disfavour that when the Prince of Wales, the eldest son of Queen Victoria, toured Canada in 1860, the colonial secretary warned Canadian authorities that the royal party would not visit towns where the Orange Order had an official role in welcoming the prince. By this time, Orangemen were so integrally involved in Canadian business and politics that they were confident they could ignore the request and proceed according to their own agenda. Resplendent in their Orange regalia, thousands showed up to greet the prince in Kingston, but were disappointed when he refused to disembark from his boat. Two days later, with no sign of surrender from the Orangemen, the prince sailed for Belleville. Word of his departure quickly spread, giving a delegation of Orangemen ample time to board a train and arrive in Belleville before him. The royal party had no choice but to continue on to the next scheduled stop in Cobourg. This time, the Orange delegation was thwarted by problems along the railway route, which, according to a report sent to Queen Victoria, had been caused by the kind of "curious accident" that sometimes took place when the government owned the rail line.[6]

Not surprisingly, there was widespread newspaper coverage of the animosity between the Orangemen and the Fenians.

In May 1864, Orangemen attacked a Corpus Christi parade in Toronto. That November, Irish Catholics celebrated Guy Fawkes Day, the anniversary of a 17th-century attempt to blow up the British parliament buildings, with a demonstration of their own. After meeting in Queen's Park, 400 men split into two companies. One marched east, one west, then, after two hours had passed, turned to salute each other with a volley of gunfire aimed towards the centre of town.[7] If nothing else, it proved that the Irish in Toronto had access to firearms, which tied in to rumours that they were stockpiling guns and ammunition in Catholic churches and cemeteries, and that some priests were secretly drilling Fenians on church property after dark.

The number of Fenians probably never exceeded more than 3,500 in all of Canada, or about 1.3 per cent of the Irish-Catholic population. Still, because they were so closely linked to the Fenians in the United States and could presumably call on them for support in the event of an armed insurrection, the danger they posed loomed extremely large in the minds of Orangemen, especially as the Fenians were fuelled by Irish nationalist rhetoric. As early as St. Patrick's Day 1863, Michael Murphy, founder of the Hibernian Benevolent Association, claimed that there were "twenty thousand thorough nationalists in Canada who would not hesitate to sacrifice their lives."[8] Three years later, Murphy reported the number as 40,000.[9]

Although the numbers were grossly exaggerated, there was definitely cause for concern about clashes between the Fenians, the Orangemen and others. In December 1864, the Orange Hall in Toronto was attacked during sectarian violence. Members of the Orange Order called for more dramatic measures to protect their ranks, but it was soon clear that the government believed regular troops, along with the militia, were equal to the task of defending the citizenry. Later that month, an alarming report reached the newspapers from Mono, a village near Orangeville (a town named after American settler Orange Lawrence, who in turn had been named in honour of the Orange Order). According to the report, on the night of December 12, several hundred Fenians converged on Mono's Presbyterian church and town hall, then set out for Orangeville "destroying everything in their way and putting all Protestants to the sword, regardless of age or sex."[10] Racing against the clock, a messenger reached Orangeville with a communiqué calling for the local "infantry company" to arm themselves and confront the Fenians.

Due to some irregularity with the orders, the militia was not called out. In the meantime, the news of the atrocities spread: "the neighborhood being alarmed, farmers and their families flocked into the village from every direction for protection, and in a few hours the streets were crowded with an affrighted populace."[11] Most of them were armed with guns or whatever else they could carry.

The attack turned out to be a total fabrication, but that discovery did not assuage the fears of the Orangemen one bit. There were calls for the formation of a Protestant militia, an idea that was quickly dismissed by the government. Besides, as the *Hamilton Evening Times* wisely editorialized, "[t]o talk of a Fenian disturbance in Canada in which only Protestants would suffer, and the Catholics escape scot free, is to talk of an impossibility."[12] Only a few weeks earlier, the *Times* had described a scenario in which a Fenian attack in Ireland would be used as a diversion to keep British troops occupied while Fenian troops in North America invaded Canada, declared the country independent, and turned it over to the United States.[13]

There were certainly enough reports from the United States to convince Canadians that an invasion would come sooner or later. After months of monitoring Fenian activity, Canadian authorities became convinced that the date would be March 17, 1866 — St. Patrick's Day. Newspaper stories offered persuasive confirmation. In November 1865, it was reported that Washington, D.C., had about 200 Fenians who were busily buying arms, uniforms, and other supplies. In January 1866, Fenians meeting in Chicago pledged two armed and equipped regiments to the cause. Later that month, noting the Detroit River was frozen, the *Times* correspondent suggested it might be time for an invasion. Clifton (now part of Niagara Falls) was put on alert when the Niagara River froze, creating an ice bridge that made it easy to move between the American and Canadian sides. In February, two volunteer companies were called up in Brockville when a Fenian attack seemed imminent.

Meanwhile, internal dissension was growing stronger among the Fenians. The faction supporting founder James O'Mahony still opposed a raid on Canada, although O'Mahony's advisors argued it would help unite the membership and raise the organization's credibility. Besides, the other faction, supporters of Union veteran General "Fighting Tom" Sweeny, was determined to attack. As late as February 2, Buffalo Fenians were reportedly opposed to the invasion, but had changed their position by the beginning of March.

On March 7, members of Hamilton's 13th Battalion and the local naval brigade were ordered to report for duty the following morning. The expected attack did not materialize. On March 9, the *Times* commented, "We are not . . . to imagine that our Canadian Ministers are a set of incapables, and that they have alarmed the country for nothing."[14]

The newspaper suggested that, while an invasion might not be imminent, a demonstration that the country was prepared for any eventuality might discourage the Fenians. Meanwhile, more defenders were called up, with an estimated 1,200 volunteers from Chatham, Woodstock, Ingersoll and elsewhere being sent to Windsor. Militia, and in some cases home guards, were called up in Ottawa, in Galt and in London.

Although most people tried to keep their normal routines, it was difficult when widespread anxiety turned everyday occurrences into enemy invasions. Early in March, friends and family of a newlywed couple in Humberstone Township, on the north shore of Lake Erie in the Niagara Peninsula, made plans to celebrate with a *charivari*, an impromptu gathering in which revellers typically made as much noise as possible until the groom bribed them into silence with alcohol. "No sooner had the disturbers of the night opened their medley of tin horns, cow-bells, and other inharmonious instruments, than the alarm spread through the neighborhood that the Fenians had arrived." A rumour quickly spread that the invaders had landed near Port Colborne and panic ensued, with people of all ages racing along the roadways or hiding in the woods, including the noisemakers who had started the whole thing![15]

As Canadians kept a wary eye on events, one of their main concerns was trying to judge the temper of the American authorities through newspaper reports. There was some conflict there. Secretary of State William Seward (who, in fact, was sympathetic to the Fenian plans) promised that the borders would be well protected by American troops. But the governor of New York, it was reported, said he would not get involved if the Fenians attacked Canada, as it was a matter for federal authorities.

As it turned out, there was no need for all the excitement. March 17 came and went without any invasion. Still, there was not much sense of relief. There were too many rumours flying about, and they continued as the spring progressed. Then, on April 13, Fenians invaded New Brunswick. They did little damage and their occupation was short-lived, thanks in part to the intervention of American authorities, who confiscated a large supply of armaments before the invaders reached their destination, as well as the presence of British navy ships. A few buildings were burned and the Union Jack was stolen from a customs house. Regarded as a prize of war, it was repeatedly displayed at Fenian rallies. The majority of the damage done was to people's sense of security. Many fled their homes, taking with them whatever belongings they could carry. Others, convinced the invaders would eventually target banks, withdrew their life savings. A sudden noise was all that was needed to send people into a frenzy.

Despite all the activity, the first invasion was a failure. Some observers were convinced the Fenians were done. But the talk of future invasions persisted. The Fenians had arms and men; some were convinced it was only a matter of time before they got their act together and pulled off a successful attack. In mid-April, the mayor of Ogdensburg, New York, crossed the St. Lawrence to visit Prescott and warn his Canadian counterpart that he had it on good authority that thousands of Fenians were on their way to his town. A Fenian flotilla was reputedly preparing to attack Picton and Belleville. In late May, a report out of Cincinnati claimed that a large shipment of arms had passed through the city and was heading northward. Fearing that a Fenian invasion was imminent, militia were put on duty along the Detroit River, especially around Sandwich (located in present-day

Windsor) and Amherstburg. On Sunday, May 27, most of the people of Sandwich were at church services when an alarm was sounded. A boatload of sightseers had set sail from the American side, bound for Sandwich and the annual Corpus Christi parade. No sooner had the vessel left port, however, than Sandwich authorities received a telegram advising them that the boat was loaded with Fenians. The residents of the town hurried to the waterfront, where they made it clear the boat would not be allowed to dock.

***

There was no doubt that the Fenians were on the move, gathering in great numbers along the New York border, as well as in Illinois. Their activities were routinely reported by a network of spies that had been set up in the aftermath of a Confederate raid on St. Albans, Vermont, in October 1864. At this point, spy networks were already in place in England and Ireland, where both the Royal Irish Constabulary and the London police had men infiltrating Fenian ranks, gathering whatever information they could. The data they collected was instrumental in stopping uprisings in both 1866 and 1867, even though it was often difficult to sort out accurate information from wildly exaggerated reports. It was rumoured, for example, that 7,000 soldiers in the British army had taken the Fenian oath in 1865, suggesting that the military was overrun with Irish republican sympathizers. The truth was more modest, but nevertheless led to about 180 courts martial between 1865 and 1869 involving Fenian sympathizers in the military.

In Canada, the Western Frontier Constabulary was created to oversee espionage activities. On December 17,

1864, President Lincoln ordered that Canadians required passports to cross into the United States. Two days later, John A. Macdonald, premier of the Province of Canada, appointed Gilbert McMicken head of the newly formed Constabulary. Born in England but raised in Scotland, McMicken had emigrated to Canada at the age of nineteen and settled in the Niagara area, where he started a freight-forwarding business. Through marriage he was connected to many of the most successful traders in the area, and it wasn't long before he parlayed his energy, intelligence and ambition into a thriving commercial and political career. By age twenty-five, he was collector of customs at Queenston, and he later became the first mayor of Clifton and then MLA for Welland. A staunch supporter of Macdonald, McMicken provided him with financial support — either a loan or outright donation — on at least one occasion, and a grateful Macdonald, who considered him "shrewd, cool and determined," did what he could to further McMicken's career. By late 1864, McMicken was living in Essex County, at the far southwestern end of the province, serving as magistrate. That November, Macdonald used his influence to have McMicken appointed excise officer in Windsor, shortly before the establishment of the Western Frontier Constabulary led to a more important position.

At first, the main activities of the Constabulary were to minimize violations of neutrality laws, whether through the actions of Confederate sympathizers or the recruitment campaigns of "substitute brokers" who paid bounties to Canadians in exchange for service in the Union army. McMicken had about two dozen men at his disposal, most of them young, physically fit and able to handle themselves in a fight. They were sent to ports and railway stations along the border with instructions to keep their eyes and ears open for any kind of suspicious activity — including, eventually, Fenian operations — and at one time or another were present in Amherstburg, Berlin (present-day Kitchener), Cobourg, Dunnville, Guelph, Hamilton, London, Paris, Port Colborne, Port Dalhousie, Port Maitland, Port Robertson, Port Stanley, St. Catharines, St. Thomas, Stratford and Toronto.

But there were a number of hurdles to overcome. McMicken's men were not necessarily suited to intelligence gathering. At one point, he had to advise them to get jobs when they were working in a community, rather than merely loitering around bars or train stations where their presence might arouse suspicion. It was not unusual for the spy network to pay for information, which meant that at least some of the intelligence provided to them was wholly or partly fabricated. Worse, although their salary was set at about thirty dollars a month, a respectable amount for the time, the agents themselves were not paid regularly and, in the early days of the Constabulary's existence, were expected to pay expenses out of their own pockets. This not only made it more difficult for agents to carry out their responsibilities but also left them open to all kinds of temptations.

Eventually the problems were worked out, and most of the agents were reasonably reliable by the time the American Civil War ended and the spies focused on the Fenians. With McMicken's blessing, a number went undercover and joined Fenian circles. Even so, the information they dug up was not always reliable and was often open to broad interpretation. Based on what he was told, Sir John Michel, commander of the British forces in Canada, was convinced that the Fenian movement was practically nonexistent in the United Province of Canada. Yet, according to McMicken's men, Fenians had active organizations in Guelph, London, Niagara Falls and elsewhere, and, according to one agent, there were nine Fenian lodges operating in Toronto in 1865.

That September, spies operating in Britain gathered enough information to stop a planned rebellion in its tracks. But events in Ireland only made the North American Fenians more determined to take action. Based on information gathered by the men of the Western Frontier Constabulary, as well as British consuls in various American cities, it appeared that there would be a Fenian attack before the year was out, and Macdonald authorized McMicken to hire another half-dozen agents. "The Fenian action in Ireland is serious," he warned. "We must not be caught napping." So great were the fears of an invasion that 10,000 militia were called out to patrol the borders. But the attack, which McMicken was convinced would take place on November 5, never materialized.

The fear of invasion did not abate, however. By early 1866, McMicken had learned that Fenian sympathizers were stockpiling weapons in a Toronto residence, and there was talk of bringing other arms into Fort Erie from Buffalo, just across the Niagara River. Piecing different bits of information together, it became apparent that the Fenians were planning an attack of some sort in Canada West for St. Patrick's Day — March 17, 1866. A week before the feast day of Ireland's patron saint, McMicken telegraphed Macdonald to tell him that 5,000 Fenians were heading for Detroit in preparation for the invasion. There were also fears that Fenians in Toronto would take action.

Again, however, the rumours proved unfounded. When the invasion of New Brunswick turned into more of a farce than a threat, McMicken concluded that much of the noise coming from the Fenian camp was harmless and primarily designed to boost morale. As far as he was concerned, repelling the invaders in New Brunswick had made it clear that Canadians did not need to fear a Fenian attack.

On May 17, McMicken wrote to John A. Macdonald, then minister of militia and attorney-general for Canada West: "I cannot conceive it within the bounds of a reasonable possibility that Sweeny will attempt any demonstrations upon Canada now."

McMicken was wrong. Two weeks later, Sweeny's men were poised to invade, with General John O'Neill leading a thousand Fenians across the Niagara River and into Canada.

CHAPTER 2
Canada West Attacked

Under cover of darkness, the Fenians slipped across the Niagara River at Buffalo, south of Black Rock, and into Canada West in the early morning hours of June 1, 1866. After cutting the telegraph lines in Fort Erie, they arrested the local men, promising they meant no harm to civilians. Instead, they announced, they had come "to strike down the oppressor's rod, to deliver Ireland from the tyrant, the despoiler and the robber." The captives were then parolled, but they did not get off entirely scot free as the invaders relied on the local residents to provide food, horses and whatever tools and equipment they required.

Some of the Fenians made their way down the Niagara River, towards Chippawa; others moved inland. Once they realized what was happening, Canadian authorities ordered a number of militia units to the Niagara Peninsula: the

Queen's Own Rifles from Toronto; the 13th Battalion out of Hamilton; and the York and Caledonia Rifles, two small companies of about fifty men each from Haldimand County. The Dunnville Naval Brigade and the Welland Field Battery were also pressed into service, travelling to Fort Erie from Port Colborne aboard a fast, steam-powered tug, the *W.T. Robb*. Miscommunication, a dearth of reliable intelligence (such as decent maps), and a lack of supplies — including essential water and food for the troops — combined with the men's inexperience and the ambitious egotism of their commanders weighed the odds heavily in the Fenians' favour. Although their numbers were roughly equal, the Fenians were almost all battle-hardened soldiers with years of experience in the American Civil War. Most of the defenders were weekend soldiers, a large number of them still in their teens. About one in three had never fired live ammunition.

When the two armies clashed on a limestone ridge slightly north of the village of Ridgeway, the defenders initially acquitted themselves well. But their inexperience was painfully evident to the Fenians. Erroneous information led Lieutenant-Colonel Alfred Booker to order a totally inappropriate defence move. Earlier reports had made it clear the Fenians had no cavalry. Most of the horses they did have had been seized from locals, and many lacked saddles. Nevertheless, at one point in the battle, someone shouted that cavalry had arrived on the field. Booker decided on a textbook defence, ordering his men to "form square," which would have been appropriate for infantry confronting cavalry. But there was no cavalry, and the formation made the Canadians even more vulnerable to enemy fire. The battle turned into a rout. In very short order, the Canadians turned and fled towards Ridgeway with the Fenians in hot pursuit, before following the railway tracks towards Port Colborne.

After some minimal looting in the village of Ridgeway, the victorious Fenians headed back towards Fort Erie, where Lieutenant-Colonel John Dennis had led the Dunnville Naval Brigade and the Welland Field Battery. Although the Fenians won a street skirmish there, British-Canadian reinforcements were pouring into the Niagara Peninsula, as American authorities simultaneously blockaded attempts to reinforce Fenian troops on the Canadian side of the river. On the morning of Sunday, June 3, the Fenians withdrew to the United States.

But they had left their mark. Nine men, all members of the Queen's Own Rifles, had been killed at Ridgeway. Others would succumb to their wounds, and many who survived would be scarred for life. There were a number of casualties from the Fort Erie skirmish as well, although, miraculously, no Canadians had been killed. It could have been far worse, given the comparative experience of the two sides, but that did not seem to matter to Canadians. Instead, there was a huge outcry of grief and anger and more than a little disbelief that the drunken, disorganized Fenians had actually done precisely what they had been threatening to do for so long.

There was also a deep sense of humiliation, although it seems never to have been expressed publicly, because the Fenians had terrified many in the Niagara Peninsula and elsewhere into fleeing for their lives. What the victims of the invasion experienced — or what they came to believe they had experienced — would deeply affect how they felt about the need for a British naval presence on the Great Lakes.

M.G. Sherk was five in June 1866, when the Fenians crossed the Niagara River and made their way inland to battle Canadian forces at Ridgeway. Half a century later, his impressions of the day remained vivid:

> My mother, alone with her children, was awakened at early dawn by the noise made by numerous vehicles passing through the village, and on going to the front door of our house that stood near the roadway, saw women and children, some of them partly dressed, huddled in wagons along with a few articles of furniture, bedding and provisions, on their way to the big marsh, a few miles back, in Humberstone Township. One of the women, wringing her hands frantically, called out to my mother: "The Fenians are coming. They are only a few miles behind. They are killing men, women and children as they go."

Some left everything behind as they hurried to safety. George Wells was the son of a Willoughby Township farmer who also did a brisk trade in horse and cattle. Banks were relatively scarce at the time, and farmers did not necessarily trust them, so the elder Wells, like a number of his contemporaries, sometimes had large sums of cash on hand. When the Fenians invaded, George watched as his father put a quantity of cash, mostly gold and silver coins, into two glass fruit jars and buried them under two feet of dirt in the root house.[1]

Like George Wells, Ernest A. Cruikshank was a young boy when the Fenians arrived. He would go on to have an illustrious military career and make a name for himself as a Canadian historian, but he never forgot the invasion of 1866. Soon after the arrival of the invaders was reported, Cruikshank's father sent him and his ploughman, John

Benner, to hide the horses rather than risk losing them to the Fenians. While they were carrying out their mission, the pair encountered Sam Johnson, a young Canadian who had served in the Union Army and had now appointed himself a kind of local Paul Revere. Mounted on a borrowed horse (which he claimed was the finest one in the peninsula) and wearing a long, mud-splattered overcoat, Johnson approached Cruikshank, his companion and a group of men and boys, only one of whom was armed. Sam's head was bare, his long, tangled hair flying in the breeze. The news he brought was frightening. According to Sam, 1,500 Fenians had landed on the Canadian shore, along with 150 pieces of cannon. Fifty years later, Cruikshank claimed that, even as a boy, he thought that number rather unbelievable, but there was more Sam told them:

> They had killed Dr. Kempson, the Reeve of Fort Erie, and all the lookout party of the Royal Canadian Rifles. My recollection is that he said he had seen their dead bodies. As he was riding down the River Road, the Fenians had fired at him and he exhibited holes in his overcoat, which he said, had been made by their bullets.[2]

No one questioned Johnson too closely, preferring instead to leave the area as quickly as possible. Cruikshank and his companion "turned westward and travelled with considerable speed without any very definite objective except to get out of the way of the blood-thirsty raiders."[3]

They were not the only ones seeking safety. Robert Larmour, a railway employee travelling through the area, witnessed dozens upon dozens of people moving along the roads as far as the eye could see, some on horseback, some in wagons, others on foot. They brought with them whatever they could carry: pots and pans, quilts, cherished pieces of furniture. For Dr. N. Brewster, who had served with the Union army, the sight appeared worse than anything he had encountered in the Civil War:

> Just at the bend of the road to the north of the village I met such a mixed and confused mass, as I have never seen elsewhere before or since. Soldiers and citizens, men, women and children, on foot and in all varieties of vehicles, with horses, cattle, sheep and pigs, all mingled together, and all hurrying along the road south.[4]

Some actually fled to the United States, reasoning that they would be safe from invaders there, but most moved inland, as far from the Niagara River as they could get. Some probably were looking for shelter with family or friends, but many almost certainly had no concrete plan except to put as much space as possible between themselves and the invaders. For some individuals, the terror was unmanageable. One man rode hell bent for leather, waving a gun in the air, until he caught up with a train that had been used to transport Canadian troops to the area. Unable to proceed any further because the train was blocking the roadway, he stopped, waving his arms about wildly, until a shot rang out. Accidentally or deliberately, he had fired his revolver directly into the roof of a railroad car. The discharge of his weapon completely undid him. He fell off his horse, babbling incoherently as he collapsed on the ground. The only words those who went to his aid could understand were "The Fenians are after me."[5]

***

In 1866, many Ontarians, along with so many others in the English-speaking world, were living the Victorian dream, putting their faith in scientific advances and technological progress and middle-class respectability. There was plenty of proof all around them of what we would call "upward mobility." Thanks to the technological marvels of the Victorian era, hard work and respectable behaviour, the descendants of penniless immigrants and the children of struggling backwoods farmers achieved prosperity and contentment.

Around 1800, it would not have been unusual for a newlywed couple starting out to have a single outfit of clothing each, and, day in and day out, to eat a simple diet consisting mostly of pork and bread, probably from the same wooden or pewter plate at every meal. It would not have been unusual if neither could read or sign their name. The gulf separating them from people who could read and write, who owned numerous garments and dishes and whose menus featured dozens of (sometimes quite elaborate) recipes was too wide for most to cross.

By the 1860s, however, growing urbanization, prosperity and education, along with stricter observance of etiquette and public morality, had brought the two sides much closer together. The Victorian middle class might never have been on an equal footing with the British aristocracy, but they could emulate the upper classes to some extent and also empathize with some of the values they held dear. When newspapers in Canada West reported that the goal of Fenians arrested in Ireland "was of the most sanguinary character . . . to strike down the nobility, the aristocracy and the land owners, and assassinate them all on the breaking out of the rebellion,"[6] residents of the province felt their own security threatened. And what made that threat even more believable was how Fenians were routinely portrayed. Inappropriate clothing, untidiness, drunkenness, violence, swearing and rude behaviour in the presence of women all reinforced the notion that the Fenians did not — and probably could not — fit into respectable society and would ultimately destroy it.

The panic in June 1866 was not solely confined to the Niagara Peninsula. One reporter crossed from the United States to Sarnia to find the town in chaos on the evening of June 2:

> Sarnia was bristling with bayonets. Such an excitement I seldom or ever witnessed. Soldiers hurrying hither and thither — their feet went tramp, tramp, tramping, and their tongues were curse, curse, cursing, the Fenians. The whole population was in a ferment, wide awake and up, in arms. I even saw several females with children in their arms.[7]

Ottawa, where the provincial parliament was gathered and which would soon become the capital of the Dominion of Canada, had all the appearance of an armed camp. Soldiers were everywhere, marching through the streets to the sound of military music or shouted commands and guarding public buildings. Although safely located some distance from the American border and so less vulnerable than many other places, Ottawa was strategically important and could not be allowed to fall into enemy hands.

Although both the Fenians and Canadian defenders continued to move about on various missions, the actual fighting was over by nightfall on June 2. What followed was an eerie silence that descended over much of the Niagara Peninsula. Cruikshank recalled that the frontier was

> almost deserted, and the inhabitants who remained kept close indoors . . . How strangely calm and quiet the night seemed to be. The death-like stillness after nine o'clock was broken only by an occasional far-away shot, the sound of galloping hoofs, or the barking of a dog.[8]

The silence continued the next morning, Sunday, June 3, at least in the Niagara area. Elsewhere in the province, the news that the Fenians had beaten Canadian troops was greeted with various reactions. In Windsor, the populace remained on alert, especially after a telegram claimed that 700 Fenians were preparing to cross the Detroit River above and below Windsor. Church services were cancelled, and within an hour, hundreds of locals carrying rifles, revolvers and shotguns were on patrol. Meanwhile, few religious services took place in Niagara, where the populace was still uncertain if it was safe to return to their homes. In Toronto, though, the streets and churches were packed as prayers were offered and hymns sung, both in remembrance of the battle casualties and in hopes that the provincial capital would continue to escape attack.

Although it was only a matter of hours before John O'Neill would lead his heavily outnumbered troops back to American soil, Canada West was still in a state of alarm as newspapers issued successive bulletins. One reported that Windsor was a "smoldering hole." Another claimed Fenians had crossed from Ogdensburg to Prescott with two regiments. Yet a third announced a Fenian armada was on its way from Chicago to Sarnia to wipe out that town.[9]

Other reports claimed the Welland Canal had been captured and Fort Erie had been put to the torch. At one point, Mr. Treble, a provincial customs officer, ran into the Fort Erie train yard screaming, "The Fenians have landed in the village and are killing everyone[!]"[10]

Ironically, a short distance away, a number of the men from Fort Erie would actually sit down and hoist a few drinks with the Fenians before the day was out. That did not mesh with the accepted image of the invaders as bloodthirsty barbarians, but it was absolutely in line with the image at least some Fenians had of themselves. The very name of the organization harked back to a time when fierce warriors were also noted for their chivalrous sense of justice and their unwillingness to harm the innocent. And, while some of them certainly were members of the loutish working-class rabble so despised by respectable Victorians, a number of them, including the officers, aspired to many of the same middle-class ideals as their critics. O'Neill certainly attempted, again and again, to stress the point that their quarrel was not with ordinary people, and the general citizenry would remain unharmed so long as they cooperated.

Getting that message out was not easy, even given the existence of Fenian newspapers. Most people more readily believed accounts in mainstream journals, but positive reports about the Fenians in these publications were few and far between. However, there were stories from credible observers that made it clear the panic was most definitely an overreaction.

George Denison was among the reinforcements sent to Niagara with the militia and later chaired committees of inquiry into the behaviour of Lieutenant-Colonels Booker and Dennis during their encounters with the Fenians. He spent at least three weeks at Fort Erie and claimed that many people had nothing but positive things to say about the invaders. Although he condemned the attack, he claimed to be "astonished" at reports of the Fenians' "good conduct." They might have confiscated food and horses, but even so, his conclusion was that "they stole but few valuables, that they destroyed, comparatively speaking, little or nothing, and that they committed no outrages on the inhabitants, but treated everyone with unvarying courtesy." After captured members of the Welland Field Battery and the Dunnville Naval Brigade were parolled, the Fenians took them to the wharf at Fort Erie, returned sidearms to officers and ended by "bidding them adieu with expressions of good will." When a group approached a widow's house in Fort Erie, asking for something to eat, the woman refused to let them inside. They laughingly replied, "very well ma[']am, we'll do here very well, it is a very nice yard," and sat down outdoors to eat the bread, milk and butter she provided. Later, a single Fenian encountered the woman, and spying a loaf of bread, picked it up to eat it. When the widow told him it was the last loaf she had, he returned it and refused to touch it again without a great deal of persuasion.

The irony of the situation was not lost on Denison. "It seems like a perfect burlesque, to see a ragged rabble without a government, country or flag, affecting chivalrous sentiments and doing acts, that put one in mind of the days of knight errantry."[11]

The image of knights errant was not the one that stuck in Canadians' minds. If anything, the popular image of the Fenians darkened considerably. It was true that the invasion of Quebec, which began June 7, was quickly repelled.

It was also true that, in many instances, a person scanning newspaper reports might get the impression that there had been no defeat at Ridgeway. Yet there was also the widespread impression that the government had been caught napping. In spite of the network of spies and the repeated warnings of an attack, the Fenians had successfully crossed into Canada and scored a victory against inadequately trained and equipped defenders. Worst of all, they had killed nine of them, mostly young men who epitomized Victorian respectability and upward mobility. William Fairbanks Tempest was a twenty-year-old medical student from Ottawa who planned to join his father's practice once he graduated. Malcolm McEachren, thirty-five, was a Scottish immigrant and father of four, a store manager who also taught Sunday school. Malcolm McKenzie, twenty-seven, was a farmer's son from Oxford County who was using his inheritance to finance his college education. The Fenians had not only put an end to their dreams and ambitions, they had also deprived Canadians of the benefits these men would bring to society.

As the summer of 1866 progressed, some argued the Fenian threat had ended, but there was much evidence to the contrary. The Fenians continued to gather in large numbers in the United States, promising to launch another invasion when the time was right. In August 1866, a Fenian picnic in Buffalo featured a sham battle. There were reports that some Fenians had actually returned to Canada, such as one from Brantford in September 1866 that claimed "the town and vicinity is swarming with strange characters, whose sneaking movements and vagabond appearance indicate that their mission is no benevolent one."[12]

Worries about a potential Fenian invasion led to a demand to cancel the provincial exhibition in Toronto, the forerunner of the Canadian National Exhibition. A number of reports strongly suggested success at Ridgeway had made the Fenians even bolder and more ruthless. One rumour claimed that Canadians in Chicago were being harassed by Fenians there.[13] Similarly, when a group of Canadian excursionists from Port Stanley visited Cleveland aboard the new steamer *City of London*, they were threatened by Fenians, many of them brandishing firearms. Although a severe storm was on the way, making it dangerous to set out on a lake voyage, the American marshal advised the Canadians to leave the safety of the harbour.[14] On another occasion, a steamer carrying Americans to Buffalo deliberately veered towards the shoreline near Ridgeway, "for the sole purpose of alarming the whole district."[15]

Whether it was accidental or not, the rancour that developed in the aftermath of Ridgeway seemed to inspire new levels of nastiness and bloody-mindedness. One Hamilton newspaper published a lengthy piece accusing the government, and especially Minister of Militia John A. Macdonald, of being "hopelessly besotted and tremendously drunk" and supported its arguments with quotations from other newspapers, including the *Perth Courier*, *Milton Champion*, Toronto's *Globe* and the *Owen Sound Advertiser*. The *Courier*'s comment was typical:

> Mr. Macdonald . . . gets drunker than usual every time the Fenians cross the border. A Fenian rumor sends him to the bottle for courage; but an actual Fenian invasion sends him to the big jug for more courage.[16]

Meanwhile, according to a rumour printed by the *New York Herald*, Canadians had formed an organization to slaughter Americans living along the border. Possibly one of the most ridiculous items of all was a "Fenian Oath" that appeared in the *Saint John's Telegraph* and was reprinted in the *Hamilton Evening Times* and presumably other newspapers. Embodying the most flamboyant Irish stereotypes of excessive religiosity, bloodthirstiness and grandiloquence, the oath invoked a variety of saints and the Virgin Mary, plus the rosary and the Catholic Church in its promise to

> fight until I die wading in fields of the red gore of the Saxon tyrants . . . And, moreover, when these English Protestants, robbers and brutes in Ireland shall be all murdered or driven into the sea, like the swine Jesus Christ caused to be drowned — we shall then embark for and take England . . .[17]

Two days after the oath was printed, a letter from Jeremiah O'Leary appeared in the newspaper, stating that no Catholic in Ireland or North America would be "so base and diabolically wicked as to take that infernal oath."[18]

Undoubtedly many readers had come to that conclusion themselves, but there were still far too many others who remained convinced that there was no atrocity the Fenians would not commit, and that since Fenians lurked everywhere, no one was safe.

Meanwhile, civilians faced danger from their own defenders, because they, too, saw the enemy around every corner. Following the June invasion in Quebec, an elderly woman was shot dead when she encountered members of the Royal Welch Fusiliers on sentry duty and failed to identify herself. According to reports, she was deaf and probably had not heard the sentries' challenge. After Ridgeway, two farmers were shot by members of the militia as they climbed a fence. They were carrying weapons the Fenians had discarded, which was apparently enough to confirm they were invaders. Not that it took much at all to arouse the defenders' suspicions. Two men from Norwich, southeast of London, went to Buffalo to buy some revolvers and then travelled to Ridgeway in search of battle souvenirs. Members of the Queen's Own Rifles spotted them and placed them under arrest for possessing "contraband of war." Although one was a justice of the peace and the other a prominent Orangeman who both went to great lengths to prove their identity, they were escorted to jail by sixty members of the militia and stayed there until the following day.[19]

Another man got into trouble because he wanted to see a Fenian up close. Bill Holly worked as a hired man for a member of the Mennonite community in southern Haldimand County. According to diarist Menlo Hoover, Holly was a bit peculiar, but an honest, hard worker who handled horses well. However, he was not one to back down from a fight, and he was too inquisitive for his own good, as Hoover recounts:

When Holly heard a rumour that there were Fenians in Dunnville, he got up early on a Saturday morning and headed east immediately after breakfast.

As he was walking over the bridge toward Dunnville he met an officer in uniform and after sizing up our friend Bill he says to him, "You're a Fenian." For an answer Bill just up with his fists and knocked him sprawling. The officer gathered himself together and ran or rode back into town for help but before he got across the bridge and before the soldiers could be mustered to gather on such short notice he met two men he knew coming from town in a buckboard. Bill told them what happened so they said, "Bill, you get in with us and we will hide you beneath the robe." They had just concealed him in time when a troop of soldiers on horses came galloping across the bridge when they drew up even they stopped and said, "Did you see anything of a Fenian on the bridge?"

"Yes. We saw one who looked different from anybody we ever saw and he was down there in the river flats running at top speed and we believe he must have been a Fenian."

With that they lost no time in hot pursuit of their man and the men in the buckboard lost no time in getting Bill away to safety. When they saw no more of the pursuers they said to Bill now you get to the woods and hide yourself until dark and then get home as fast as possible and we wish you luck.

Bill arrived home about 4 o'clock in the morning and hungry as a bear.[20]

Just the hint of Fenian sympathies could also create trouble, as an incident in Stratford demonstrated. A customer, Mrs. Ann Dawe, claimed a local store owner, J. Corcoran, "seemed to exult" in the killing and wounding of members of the Queen's Own Rifles at Ridgeway. Mrs. Dawe took offense, left the store saying she would never return and then discussed the incident at another store. Claiming her story was erroneous, Corcoran threatened to sue, and Mrs. Dawe issued a convoluted apology, which was printed in the local newspaper and elsewhere. The incident showed how easily careless remarks arising from anti-Fenian sentiments could create problems for ordinary people.

Meanwhile, the authorities took measures to minimize any further damage from invaders. On June 8, the provincial legislature met in Ottawa for the first time. Its first order of business was to suspend *habeas corpus*, one of the fundamental civil rights enjoyed by British subjects. While this meant that suspects could be taken into custody with very little proof of wrongdoing and incarcerated without trial indefinitely, most Canadians were willing to risk potential civil rights abuses in exchange for national security. Among them was senior civil servant Edmund Merdeith, who witnessed enactment of the bill from the parliamentary gallery. "A very great satisfaction expressed," he noted in his diary.

That may have been the opinion held by the majority, at least at first. Slowly, however, the government became aware of just how much harm the paranoia surrounding the invasions was causing. On June 21, John A. Macdonald, acting in his capacity as attorney-general of Canada West, published a circular warning against arbitrary arrests. Even if an individual was known to belong to the Fenians, it was imperative that no one be taken into custody without solid evidence of treason or other serious crimes. Too many arrests had already been made, causing considerable upset among Irish-Canadians, who felt themselves besieged. As the summer of 1866 wore on, it seemed more and more difficult to know who to trust. And that not only applied to nearby friends and neighbours. It also applied to the Americans to the south.

CHAPTER 3
Dealing with the Neighbours

The Fenian invasion was just one of the reasons why British gunboats would be welcomed so warmly when they reached the Great Lakes late in the summer of 1866. To understand Canadians' reaction to the gunboats, it is also necessary to understand the world in which they lived. On the one hand, there was much to celebrate. The colonies that would unite as the Dominion of Canada on July 1, 1867, were moving steadily out of the pioneer era and into the industrial age. Near miraculous progress was taking place in transportation and communication as railways spread across the landscape like so many iron spider webs, followed closely by telegraph lines, both of which contributed to the explosive growth of newspapers. Although Jules Verne would not publish *Around the World in 80 Days* until 1873, the novel captured the essence of what had been occurring in travel. The book was not science fiction so much as mildly speculative fiction based on technology that was already in use by the early 1860s. And, while it would be another century before the term *global village* became popular, the world was already "shrinking" at a rate that, to some at least, was alarming.

At the same time they were hailed as signs of progress, railways, telegraphs and newspapers presented a triple threat to the peace and contentment of Canadians, as well as other Westerners. Trains made the transportation of goods and people faster and easier, but they also provided a means by which unwelcome immigrants or invaders could be moved rapidly. Because day-to-day business increasingly relied on rail transport for the goods and materials required by Victorian society, railways were a natural target for anyone wishing to cause disruption or damage. The telegraph allowed the rapid transmission of information, making it possible to quickly mobilize troops if an invasion threatened or to summon aid after a major fire or natural disaster. But telegraph lines were not secure, so anyone who was able to climb a pole and knew Morse code could tap into a line. Unless the message was encrypted, the interceptor could then discover details, such as the activities of defenders, that might tip the scale in favour of invaders. Furthermore, telegraphed messages were not always complete or accurate. Sometimes they were little more than rumours that might send the populace into a panic. And, with the successful installation of the transatlantic telegraph cable in 1866, that panic might have had its origins in events taking place thousands of miles away.

Both railways and telegraphs had profound influence on newspapers, making it possible for news from London, England, the financial and military epicentre of the world, to reach a reader on the shores of the Great Lakes within a couple of days, occasionally sooner. Although that seems glacially slow to anyone accustomed to the instant communication made possible by 21st-century social media such as Twitter and YouTube, it was amazingly, even frighteningly, fast for Victorians. A single, distant incident, such as an armed uprising in Ireland, could set a reader in Toronto trembling, and not just because of the horror any violent action arouses in sane individuals, regardless of the era in which they live. Newspaper editors and publishers were much more likely to print sensational reports without confirming facts, especially when they could boost sales or scoop a rival. Retractions or corrections could always be printed later, with little risk of libel suits or other legal sanctions. Newspaper readers, however, often took such reports to heart as gospel truth, especially if the publisher's political views coincided with the reader's own.

As the 19th century progressed, newspapers had grown by leaps and bounds thanks to increased literacy levels and the rise of the middle class. They were pored over, especially during long evenings when there was not much else to do except read, sew, play parlour games or make music. Their contents were discussed at length. A single report of a specific incident in Ireland would be understood by a hypothetical Toronto reader in the context of a broader frame of reference, one that included many stories, not necessarily fair or accurate, about Irish issues and the hazards they posed for ordinary Canadians, or even ordinary Englishmen and Australians. Because of their immediacy, newspapers made it possible for readers to see how distant events could affect activities closer to home. Together, newspapers, telegraphs and railroads shaped

Canadians' understanding of the world. And crucial to that understanding was insight into the American psyche and how the political and commercial ambitions of the United States might ultimately affect Canada.

In late October 1864, Thomas D'Arcy McGee was one of the many delegates gathered in Quebec to discuss plans for Confederation. Among the arguments supporting a union of British North American colonies was the threat posed by the United States, one McGee described eloquently and dramatically with a thumbnail history of American expansionism:

> They coveted Florida, and seized it; they coveted Louisiana, and purchased it; they coveted Texas, and stole it; and then they picked a quarrel with Mexico, which ended by their getting California. They sometimes pretended to despise these colonies as prizes beneath their ambition; but had we not had the strong arm of England over us we should not now have a separate existence.[1]

When the American Civil War ended, British North America was a small collection of colonies spread along a narrow border, south of which lay a somewhat hostile neighbour populated by thousands of newly idle soldiers. Although many Canadians had fought with the Union army in the war, Britain was officially neutral. Even so, some Britons surreptitiously supported the Confederate cause, in part because the Confederate states provided the cotton upon which British textile mills depended. When it became apparent that a loophole in British legislation allowed for the construction of Confederate ships in British shipyards and the separate supply of arms, there were some who quickly took advantage. Two British-built boats, the *Florida* and the *Alabama*, inflicted considerable damage on the North: In a two-year period, the *Alabama* sank sixty-nine merchantmen valued at more than $6 million.[2]

This was not the only source of friction, either. On November 8, 1861, the Union vessel *San Jacinto*, commanded by Captain Charles Wilkes, accosted the British packet ship *Trent* as it made its way out of Havana, bound for England. On board were two Confederate envoys, John Sidell and James M. Mason, who were heading to Europe to obtain official diplomatic recognition of the Confederate states. Wilkes, who already had a reputation for impulsiveness and rash action, decided that the Confederates could be considered contraband and that it was his duty to prevent them from reaching their destination. After signalling the *Trent*, he fired a warning shot across her bow, which resulted in the packet displaying British colours but otherwise ignoring the American vessel. Wilkes promptly had a shell fired directly in the *Trent*'s path, which brought her to a halt. The Americans then sent a boarding party to the British ship and took Sidell and Mason into custody, along with their secretaries, then transported them to prison in Fort Warren, Boston. A diplomatic tempest erupted, with the British describing Wilkes's actions as an outrage and an act of piracy, and France supporting Britain's stance. The general attitude of the American public, as reflected in the press, was that the British had no cause for complaint given their repeated violations of neutrality. The Americans ignored demands that the envoys be released and that the United States apologize, even though Britain warned that failure to comply would result in a declaration of war, with Canada as the battleground.

The military in Canada was put on alert. Meanwhile, 14,000 troops were sent to the colony to beef up defences. The Americans waited as long as possible before releasing the envoys, but took the position that Wilkes had been acting without official orders and did not issue an apology. Disaster was averted, but the crisis was a dramatic reminder of how vulnerable Canada was and how potentially dangerous her neighbour to the south.

Two more incidents during the Civil War further strained relations between the United States and Britain and the North American colonies. On December 7, 1863, sixteen passengers aboard the American merchant vessel *Chesapeake* took over the boat, killing one crew member and injuring others. Although ostensibly operating under letters of marque from the Confederacy, a number of the mutinous passengers were actually Maritimers, at least seven of them residents of New Brunswick. They took the *Chesapeake* to Nova Scotia.

Americans condemned the capture of the *Chesapeake* as one more example of British high-handedness, even though the majority of British North Americans had no sympathy for what they considered an act of piracy. This did not prevent the Americans from recapturing the ship in Canadian waters. The uproar eventually faded with little lasting effect, except the lingering memory of yet another disagreement between friendly nations.

The next uproar came in October 1864, when a group of twenty-one Confederate sympathizers in civilian clothes raided St. Albans, Vermont. Led by a twenty-one-year-old theology student from Kentucky, Bennet H. Young, the sympathizers stole $200,000 from local banks and killed one man. They also stole horses from local citizens and bombarded some of their targets with Greek fire, spreading panic through the border towns. A posse of locals pursued the raiders across the border into Canada, eventually capturing fourteen of them.

Canadian police magistrate Charles Coursol was sent to Saint-Jean, on the Richelieu River, to preside over the case but soon changed the venue to Montreal. Coursol was apparently out of his depth, as he ignored the crucial question: whether the St. Albans raiders were common criminals or commissioned officers of the Confederacy. Nor did he seek the advice of more knowledgeable legal minds. Instead, he dismissed the case on a technicality on December 13, noting that the crimes had been committed in the United States and so were beyond his jurisdiction. The prisoners were set free.

American outrage knew no bounds, and many Canadians were angered as well. John A. Macdonald called Coursol a "wretched prig of a police magistrate," and Coursol was dismissed from office on January 26, although he was later reinstated. Meanwhile, the United States called for immediate retaliation. The comment of the *Janesville Gazette* was typical of American sentiment: "Our kind-hearted and disinterested neighbors . . . intend to remain so very neutral that rebel thieves and murderers are assured of protection and an asylum within their borders."[3] Obviously, the Americans could not tolerate that situation. General John Adams Dix, former secretary of state for New York and the highest ranking major-general of the Union volunteers, issued orders authorizing Americans to pursue such wrongdoers across the border if necessary and capture them in Canada. It did not seem to matter to Dix that, in doing so, the Americans would be crossing an international border. Meanwhile, a number of American newspapers called for an immediate invasion, creating such consternation in both Canada East and Canada

West that the militia was mobilized to guard the frontier between the two countries. American anger was so great that Secretary of State William Seward invoked a clause that would nullify the Rush-Bagot Agreement after six months. The treaty had been signed in 1817, in the aftermath of the War of 1812, and limited armed naval vessels on the Great Lakes and Lake Champlain. On the Great Lakes, each side was allowed a total of three vessels (one on Lake Ontario, two on the other lakes), each armed with one eighteen-pound cannon.[4] Although the United States cancelled plans to end the agreement before the six months were up, the very fact that they were considering the action underscored the volatile relations between the two countries.[5]

Ramping up Canadians' fears of attack sanctioned by the United States government was the awareness of the American philosophy of "manifest destiny," the same idea McGee had referred to in his 1864 speech. The term was coined in 1845 by newspaperman John O'Sullivan to support American annexation of Oregon and Texas. But the gospel it represented — that the divinely decreed fate of the people of the United States was to completely fill the continent — had been part of the American psyche far longer. Former President Thomas Jefferson invoked the spirit of manifest destiny in August 1812, when he declared that the conquest of Canada would be "a mere matter of marching" and result in "the final expulsion of England from the American continent."[6] And, even earlier, future President John Quincy Adams had written, "The whole continent of North America appears to be destined by Divine Providence to be peopled by one nation, speaking one language, professing one general system of religious and political principles, and accustomed to one general tenor of social usages and customs. For the common happiness of them all, for their peace and prosperity, I believe it is indispensable that they should be associated in one federal Union."[7]

As of 1866, by fair means or foul, Americans had acquired territory from Spain, Mexico, France, and numerous Native tribes. They had also begun the discussions that would eventually lead to the Alaska Purchase, which had its roots in Russian efforts to limit British power in the northwest. After the Civil War, traumatic memories of the fighting, the widespread destruction of property and a population swollen by both reproduction and immigration combined to push Americans into new territory. Most of them headed west, but there were also some who looked northward. An example of their interest in Canada is revealed by discussions surrounding compensation for damages caused by British-built Confederate warships, the *Florida* and *Alabama*. At one point in the negotiations, the Americans suggested they might be willing to accept as payment the colony of Nova Scotia, the Red River settlement (now Winnipeg) and part of British Columbia.[8]

While diplomatic relations with the United States remained generally civil, if not friendly, a certain wariness always existed. In preparing for the possibility of a Fenian invasion, British and Canadian authorities constantly had to hedge their bets about the likely behaviour of American authorities. There was widespread belief that the United States would not lift a finger to stop Fenian incursions, and some feared they might actively encourage them. There was also the possibility that the Americans might not have the power to stop the Fenians, a matter British commander Sir John Michel discussed in a March 1866 letter to Governor-General Lord Monck:

It would appear that their organization in the States daily gathers strength in men and money, and shows a more audacious disregard of what may be the intentions of the United States' Government; and it appears to me that if that Government puts off much longer decided action it becomes very doubtful whether the moment will not have become too powerful for them, under their existing weakness, to cope with.[9]

In the aftermath of the 1866 raids, however, military authorities in Canada were generally satisfied that their neighbours to the south had acted responsibly. Both Monck and Michel expressed confidence in Americans' willingness to keep the Fenians in check, although there were still some misgivings about their ability to effectively do so. Writing to the secretary of state for war on June 4, 1866, just after the Battle of Ridgeway, Michel said, "in my estimation, the action of the United States Government has staved off a serious invasion . . . The U.S. Government is seizing arms and apparently acting in good faith, but it is not sufficiently strong entirely to prevent invasion."[10]

Monck was more sanguine. Writing to Edward Cardwell, British secretary of state for the colonies, a few days later, he enclosed a proclamation from the American president and an order from the American attorney-general calling for the arrest of Fenians. In his opinion, the United States was "exerting itself in an energetic manner" to stop the Fenians and "all real danger" had passed.

Yet there was no doubt that many American politicians relied heavily on the Irish vote and did not care to offend the Fenians too deeply. Even after the invasions of 1866 proved the Fenians meant business, they continued to hold "indignation meetings," conferences and rallies in the United States. There were reports that they continued to gather armaments. In May 1867, for instance, the *New York Herald* claimed that a city rifle manufacturer had been producing 1,600 rifles a week since January and had hinted that they were meant for the Fenians.[11]

American authorities dealt leniently with Irish-Americans who invaded Canada in 1866, in many instances covering their transportation costs from the border back to large American cities. Relatively few were taken into custody for violation of neutrality laws, and many avoided imprisonment altogether. Those who did receive jail terms were almost invariably released before their sentences were up, usually right before an election. And the Americans did not confine their interest solely to the invaders who made their way back to the United States. The fate of those captured in Ontario and Quebec in June 1866 was of particular concern.

Eighty-one Fenians had been captured at Ridgeway, sixty-five of them in Ontario. They became the target of Canadians' outrage, anger and shock. A.A. Davis of the York Rifles was one of those assigned to escort prisoners from Niagara to Toronto in the aftermath of Ridgeway and Fort Erie. Writing to his wife on June 6, he described the welcome they received:

> Left Fort Erie yesterday morning escorting six (6) prisoners with whom I had to proceed to Toronto. I arrived at about 5 o'clock and took them to the gaol. The greatest excitement you ever saw. The people wanted to take the prisoners and lynch them. I had to charge bayonets on them, and get an escort of cavalry.[12]

Outraged citizenry, including politicians, called for nothing less than the death penalty for the Fenian prisoners. Reporting on public opinion in Toronto, the *London Free Press* revealed that the "general feeling in the city is to execute the whole gang forthwith" and that the "scamps fully expect a hemp neck tie."[13] Hamilton-area politician Joseph Rymal caught something of the temper of the times when he remarked in the legislature that he "looked upon the Fenians as half human hyenas, who should be hunted down without mercy."[14] "Honest Joe," who was known for his sense of humour, was almost certainly joking in an effort to bring a little bit of perspective to the situation, but for many it was no laughing matter. Thomas D'Arcy McGee, who had once worked for the same cause as the invaders, was adamant that they deserved to hang, although he would later temper his remarks for political expedience. Although it would be October 1866 before the Fenians came to trial, both the British and American governments made it plain early on that they would be watching events carefully. Many of the Fenians had been born in Ireland and, as British citizens, their participation in the invasion made them guilty of treason. While the penalty for treason was death, it was not always imposed. Three decades earlier, as a result of the 1837 rebellion, only two men had been executed in what was then Upper Canada, although a number were imprisoned or exiled. By 1866, British and Canadian society had changed dramatically, influenced by ideas of equality, responsible government and liberalism, which made capital punishment for political crimes even more abhorrent. Beyond that, the British government recognized that the very last thing it needed to do was create new Fenian martyrs, whose deaths might inspire their comrades to further military action.

Meanwhile, the Americans opposed capital punishment for reasons of their own, most notably because some of the Fenian invaders were naturalized American citizens. In some cases, their status was not clear, but the American stance was that no American blood would be shed, not even as a result of a fair judicial process. Coverage of the trials, along with stories of continued Fenian activities in the United States, ensured that Canadians would continue to focus on the Fenian threat for many months after June 1866. Each newspaper report provided another opportunity for readers to remember the invasions and the anxious months leading up to them, again reinforcing their fears. While it might not have been the best idea in the world to keep the populace on the edge of panic, there was definite political payoff involved. Deliberately or not, between memories of the 1866 invasions, reports of continued Fenian activity hinting at future invasions and a widespread distrust of American motivation, pro-Confederation politicians had a useful arsenal in their fight for Canadian unity. In New Brunswick in particular, public opinion shifted in favour of Confederation largely because of the Fenian invasions. And, as arrangements for Confederation solidified, there was considerable concern about Canadian defences. The gunboats would provide some reassurance that measures were being taken in that department.

CHAPTER 4
Improvising a Navy

Soon after news of the Fenian attack on Niagara reached military authorities, militia units were sent to defend the area. By the evening of June 1, 1866, the Queen's Own Rifles of Toronto and the 13th Battalion of Hamilton had rendezvoused in Port Colborne, the terminus of the Welland Canal on Lake Erie. Both were commanded by ambitious, overconfident militia officers whose lack of combat experience did little to deflate their dreams of military glory. Almost immediately, Lieutenant-Colonel Alfred Booker of the 13th seized command. John Dennis, commander of the Queen's Own, held the same rank; like Booker, he had been made lieutenant-colonel in 1858. But Booker's commission had been issued a short time earlier, which was all the justification he needed to put himself in charge. In spite of his relative lack of experience, he had a brigade at his disposal, a command normally reserved for a general.

Colonel George Peacocke, the British regular charged with defending the Niagara Peninsula, had laid out a plan whereby Booker would take his troops overland, while Dennis would put his men aboard the ferry steamer *International* and patrol the Niagara River from Fort Erie to Chippawa, just above Niagara Falls. With luck, the two groups would trap the Fenian invaders between them. But the *International* did not show up as expected; her owners, the Buffalo & Lake Huron Railway, had put her in to port rather than risk any damage to their property. For a while, it seemed Dennis's chances for military fame would disappear like so much cannon smoke. But then he and Booker recalled what they had learned earlier that day.

In April 1865, Lachlan McCallum had written to Minister of Militia John A. Macdonald, offering to lease a boat to the government for the defence of the Great Lakes:

> Having understood that the Government intends placing one or two Boats on Lake Erie for the purpose of preventing Raids and as I have a Boat similar to those employed by the Americans last season, only a much stronger and better one, but not of more warlike appearance. Built in the spring of 1864 . . . and would carry two guns. I would like to charter said boat to the government.[1]

McCallum was referring to the *W.T. Robb*, a tug that had been built at his Stromness shipyard by George Hardison of Buffalo. Measuring 120' long, 20'10" wide and 10' deep, she was launched April 26, 1864, and was considered one of the fastest boats on Lake Erie. Although she had a promising future as a commercial vessel, as his letter indicates, McCallum also saw some excellent possibilities to profit by putting her into government service. And McCallum was not likely to give up easily once he saw this kind of opportunity. Experience had taught him how much could be accomplished through determination and persistence. Born in Tyree, Argyleshire, Scotland, in 1823, McCallum had arrived in Canada in his late teens and set about building both a commercial fortune and a political career. Eventually, he had a store; a fleet of tugs carrying lumber, grain and other cargo; and a shipyard. Although he failed to win election to the legislature of Canada West in 1863, he would win a seat in the Ontario legislature in 1871 and receive an appointment to the Senate in 1885. In the meantime, he focused on a number of other interests, including the defence of Lake Erie — which also meant the protection of his own vessels and cargoes.

In 1863, McCallum established the Dunnville Naval Brigade. Many of the members were friends or colleagues who were involved in local water transportation, including Montrose Galbraith, a customs officer on the Feeder Canal; Francis Lattimore, who captained McCallum's boat *Scottish Chief*; and Walter T. Robb, who would captain the eponymous *W.T. Robb*. Ambitious and energetic, McCallum, who served as captain of the organization, wanted his brigade to be outstanding. Not only did he drill his men regularly, he also paid for their uniforms out of his own pocket. Dressed in blue with silver buttons, the Dunnville Naval Brigade was quite impressive, although McCallum clearly saw room for improvement. In his letter to Macdonald, he explained that, along with other lake sailors, the members of the naval brigade could be used to crew the gunboat he was proposing to lease. "Said Company has been formed three years, partially understand the drill and used to the water and the working of a Boat."[2]

Never one to hold back on a topic he felt he understood, McCallum also offered the future prime minister some advice on effective and economical naval defence:

> I am of the opinion that twenty or thirty men placed on a Boat in this way would be a better prevention against Raids than five or six companies as they can move from point to point when required so to do. And the expenses will be a small comparison to that of keeping five or six companys [sic].[3]

Macdonald did not take up McCallum's offer, but when the Fenians invaded in 1866, John Dennis certainly saw the advantage in using the *Robb* in place of the missing *International*. Around 10:30 on the night of June 1, he telegraphed McCallum, instructing him to bring the Dunnville Naval Brigade to Port Colborne, where the boat would pick up members of the Welland Field Battery. By 2 a.m. on June 2, the *Robb* was on its way eastward, arriving in Port Colborne at 4 a.m.

As the sun climbed higher on what would become a lovely summer day, the *Robb* chugged towards the Niagara River. Once there, all the men except for one officer in civilian clothes were ordered below deck, in hopes that the Fenians would assume the *Robb* had no military mission. Over the next few hours, men were sent ashore to patrol the Canadian countryside and capture any Fenians they might encounter. This they accomplished, and the Fenian prisoners were put aboard the *Robb*.

In the meantime, the Fenians had defeated Booker's troops at the Battle of Ridgeway. Nine Canadians were killed in action or died soon after the battle, while another thirty-seven were wounded and close to two dozen of them would succumb to their wounds. In comparison, fewer than half a dozen Fenians were killed and sixteen were wounded. After the battle ended, the Fenians chased the Canadians back to the village, where the panicked militiamen followed the railway tracks to Port Colborne. Rather than giving chase, the Fenians engaged in a brief period of minor looting, then reassembled and started back towards the Niagara River. Word of the Fenian victory spread among the populace of the peninsula, among whom was a War of 1812 veteran named Lewis Palmer, now in his seventies, who lived two miles west of Fort Erie. Palmer was among those who told Dennis that the main body of Fenians was approaching Fort Erie. More than that, the elderly veteran had sized up the enemy force and bluntly advised Dennis that he was so badly outnumbered he had only one course of action: get his men onto the *Robb* and out of the area as quickly as possible.

Dennis refused to believe Palmer or anyone else, seemingly unable to grasp the concept of a Fenian success. Although he temporarily allowed himself to be convinced and got the men back aboard the *Robb*, he then changed his mind and put them ashore once more. Soon afterwards, when about 800 Fenians swarmed in from the west, Lachlan McCallum and several men of the Dunnville Naval Brigade, along with members of the Welland Field Battery, were standing in two lines close to Fort Erie harbour.

The moment the Fenians began firing, Dennis ducked

and ran for cover. "Where the Hell are you going?" McCallum shouted after him, but he had no time to discover the answer or follow. He and the rest of the men on shore were too busy returning fire. Meanwhile, Captain Robb had assessed the situation and, determined not to let his boat fall into enemy hands, sailed out of the harbour to the middle of the river. From that position, the men who had remained aboard provided what cover they could for their comrades on shore. All the while, Americans spectators on the eastern shore of the Niagara River watched the proceedings, many of them cheering on the Fenians.

The brief and bloody encounter dissolved into a battle that moved through the streets of Fort Erie. Although no Canadians were killed, several were wounded and forty were captured. One Fenian was killed and fourteen were wounded. As for the *Robb*, she came under heavy fire from the Fenians assembled on the Canadian side. Bullets slammed into the wheelhouse, the cabin and the bulwarks, but Captain Robb remained coolly at the wheel, navigating the tug through nearly a mile of deadly lead. Throughout the ordeal, his close friend and employer Lachlan McCallum (who had been rescued from the shore by Robb) stood by, ready to take over the wheel if Robb fell. Miraculously, neither was wounded. By 6:30 that evening, they were back in Port Colborne.

Unfazed by the events of the day, McCallum was eager to return to the Niagara River and face the Fenians again. Instead, the *Robb* was ordered to stay at Port Colborne and protect the harbour from any possible attack. By the time the tug steamed back to Fort Erie on Sunday, June 3, the town was safely in Canadian hands. Meanwhile, in other towns on the Great Lakes and along the St. Lawrence River, British and Canadian authorities had hastily cobbled together a navy.

***

While the threat of an invading army was the primary focus for Canada's defenders, it was impossible to overlook the need for adequate naval defences. Time and time again there had been reports that the Fenians were forming a navy of some variety. According to one rumour, after a victory in eastern Canada, they hoped to set up a government and issue letters of marque to authorize privateers — legalized pirates — to prey on British ships. In order to cross into Canada in June 1866, they had depended on ships and barges, and, ultimately, their withdrawal was a direct result of naval manoeuvres. By stopping reinforcement and supplies from reaching O'Neill's army on the Canadian side, the American authorities had forced his retreat.

Canada had no navy of her own, and there were no immediate plans to create one even after Confederation. Yet there was no denying the importance of control of the Great Lakes and the rivers connecting to them. The British had known control was crucial as early as the Seven Years' War, when they constructed a dockyard at Fort Oswego on Lake Ontario in an attempt to build vessels that would attack the French Fort Niagara. The plan failed, but after the onset of the American Revolution, the British established a naval presence, partly to provide defence against the former colonies to the south, but mostly to provide transportation and protection for commerce. When the War of 1812 began, both sides quickly realized the outcome would depend on who controlled the lakes, and a race to build the swiftest, most capable warships ensued. The loss of Lake Erie after Oliver Perry's victory at Put-in-Bay in September 1813 was a severe blow to the British, resulting in the abandonment of the southwestern part of what was then Upper Canada. For a time, it also seemed that the British would pull their land forces as far east as Kingston, too, with results that can only be imagined.

When peace was restored, one of the first issues to be addressed, through the Rush-Bagot Agreement, was a limitation on armed vessels on the lakes. Meanwhile, naval establishments were constructed at Port Maitland near the mouth of the Grand River in 1815 and at Penetanguishene on Georgian Bay in 1816. Ease of navigation, sheltered harbours and a ready supply of timber for shipbuilding were the main factors influencing the choice of these locations. By the 1840s, however, both had been abandoned. When the American Civil War began and British-American relations deteriorated, steps were taken to provide some measure of defence for the Great Lakes. One of these was the creation of naval brigades.

The militia act in Canada West in 1862 resulted in the creation of seven of these naval brigades. Five were on Lake Ontario, located at Hamilton, Oakville, Toronto, Kingston, and Garden Island (two miles south of Kingston). Two were on Lake Erie: at Port Stanley, south of London, and at Dunnville, a short distance upstream from Port Maitland, the site of one of the abandoned naval establishments. About sixty men, preferably experienced sailors, were expected to form each brigade, which was to be ready when called to man whatever vessels could be acquired for defence. Although some provision was made for the supply of uniforms and equipment, these were never adequate, and, in the winter in particular, carrying out the requisite naval drills was not always easy. In 1865, British legislation impacted naval defence in Canada West by stipulating that colonies could put into service "vessels of war,"[4] with the understanding that whatever crew was attached to these vessels would be regarded as members of the Royal Navy if a crisis arose.[5] Although the Rush-Bagot Agreement was still in effect, both the British and Americans got around that inconvenience by reassuring each other that armed vessels on the Great Lakes were primarily to protect each country from internal threats, rather than an external enemy.

But now there was an external enemy to be considered, and it had easy access to Canadian targets. In March 1866, a Royal Navy captain named Bythesea travelled from Washington, D.C., to visit the United Province of Canada and noted that the distance between Montreal and Kingston covered 210 miles. Although the first ninety miles were entirely within Canadian territory, west of that, the St. Lawrence formed the border between Canada and the United States, a narrow ribbon of water that could be crossed easily in the event of attack. Bythesea envisioned the placement of a collection of boats along the river, at various strategic locations, including Lake St-Louis and Lake St-Francis, in part to protect nearby canals. In the fifty years since the War of 1812, canals and railroads had revolutionized transportation in Canada. First, the canals offered better water routes than those provided by natural streams, because they were shorter, more easily navigated or avoided impassable obstacles such as Niagara Falls. Railways, because they were not dependent on streams in the same way, were more revolutionary yet. But both were vulnerable to attack. Some well-placed explosives or an energetic work crew with the right tools could bring movement of men and materiel to a grinding halt in very short order. This meant that naval defences were essential.

Discussing the issue with Vice-Admiral Sir James Hope,

Canada's Governor-General Lord Monck argued that nothing but gunboats would "efficiently and inexpensively" protect the border. "The fact of the existence of such craft on the St. Lawrence will have the most powerful deterrent influence on the minds of those who contemplate crossing with evil intentions, because it will reduce to a minimum the chance of their ever returning in safety."[6]

Lord Monck had been appointed governor-general of the Province of Canada in 1861 and would become the first governor-general of the new dominion in 1867. A member of the Anglo-Irish aristocracy, Monck was born in Templemoore, Ireland, and was educated at Trinity College, Dublin, where he earned a law degree. Initially, he appeared to be a rather mediocre politician and left politics after three years in office, following a Liberal defeat at the polls.

Although he had extensive landholdings in Ireland, Monck was chronically in need of cash and for this reason accepted various appointments, including his post in Canada. He arrived in November 1861, in the midst of the *Trent* affair. Unlike many of his countrymen, he had considerable sympathy for the North in the American Civil War, and this shaped his actions to some extent. He also relied on a number of astute advisors and had the sense to use their expertise, especially regarding the usefulness of gunboat diplomacy. His March 1866 letter makes it clear that he understood the impact an appearance of naval strength could have on Fenians' plans for invasions, and he repeatedly returned to that theme throughout the ensuing troubles.

When the Fenians invaded Niagara, the Canadian Ministry of Marine scrambled to find suitable vessels to defend the coastal waters. According to a government report of late 1867, a total of fifteen boats were leased or purchased between June 1866 and November 1, 1867: *Metamoras*, *St. Andrew*, *Hercules #1*, *Royal*, *Rescue*, *Hercules #2*, *Magnet*, *Watertown*, *Michigan/Prince Alfred*, *Lione*, *Gordon*, *British America*, *W.T. Robb*,[7] *Satellite* and *Canada*.[8]

Several of the boats were in service for about three weeks and then returned to their owners once the most serious danger had passed. Others were kept in service for a longer period, notably *St. Andrew* and *Royal*, while *Rescue* and *Michigan*, both initially leased, were eventually purchased.[9]

Aside from the *Robb* — which may not have been officially sanctioned by the government until after the fact — three boats immediately put into service were the *Royal*, chartered on June 2, and the *Hercules* and *Canada*, chartered on June 3. These were armed with guns from two British ships stationed in eastern Canada,[10] the *Pylades* and *Aurora*, and put into service as quickly as possible. In the case of the *Royal*, it took two days before it started patrolling the St. Lawrence near Cornwall,[11] by which time the *Robb* had already returned to a hero's welcome in Port Colborne and the *Rescue* was en route from Toronto to Windsor.

The *Rescue* was a three-decked wooden sloop with a double engine and a heavy hull. Measuring 121' long, 23' wide and 10' deep, she had a registered tonnage of 248.38 and was equipped with two engines with a combined 100 horsepower.[12] Fuelled by coal or wood, she was able to reach between eleven and twelve miles per hour, "a fine speed."[13] In addition, she could travel through all the canals and rivers between Fort William (now Thunder Bay) and Quebec City, as well as accommodate between 200 and 250 troops if necessary.

On June 3, the Toronto Naval Brigade had received orders to prepare to sail for Windsor aboard her. In short order, her crew had loaded sixty-seven tons of coal and also readied the ship for any hostile encounters with the installation of a 32-pounder cannon on the main deck. Although it was somewhat too big for the boat, the gun was mounted in such a way that it could fire in any direction necessary.

The crew consisted of slightly more than sixty men, under the command of Captain W.F. McMaster. Serving as sub-lieutenant was Edmund B. VanKoughnet, a seventeen-year-old midshipman attached to the British warship *Aurora*, which was then stationed in Quebec. VanKoughnet came from a Loyalist family with a strong military tradition. His father, Phillip, was a lawyer and politician who had been appointed chancellor of Court of Chancery of Upper Canada in 1862, a position he would hold until his death in 1869. Edmund had been on leave in Toronto when the Fenians invaded. He immediately telegraphed for and received permission to temporarily join the crew of the *Rescue*.

On June 5, it looked like VanKoughnet and his shipmates might see some action, just as the *Robb* had. As they made their way westward on Lake Erie, an unidentified vessel was spotted, belching "heavy clouds of black smoke" as she headed for the *Rescue* at full speed. Aware of rumours of a Fenian flotilla on the lake, the crew prepared to engage:

> The men were called to quarters, the 32-pounder loaded and charged with chain-shot, and every preparation made to give battle in case the approaching steamer should happen to be a foe. As it came nearer it was seen that she was a side-wheeler . . . Jack Fields (an experienced gunner) took charge of the 32-pounder, which he carefully trained on the stranger . . . All were now expectant and ready for action, awaiting orders

to fire. But as the steamer approached closer it was learned that she was the United Sates revenue cutter "Fessenden," which was on patrol duty on Lake Erie.[14]

The American crew was also on the lookout for Fenians and initially believed the *Rescue* was one of their boats. Fortunately, matters were quickly settled, Captain W.F. McMaster and his American counterpart exchanged courtesies and the *Rescue* steamed away.

The remainder of her voyage was far from peaceful. About midnight, around the time the *Rescue* was passing Port Stanley, she ran into a heavy storm. Deluged by torrential rain and buffeted by high winds, she pitched and rolled on heavy seas. The 32-pounder was in danger of breaking loose and smashing anything it encountered. Round shot, which had been piled on deck for easy access, was pushed out of restraining frames by the boat's motion in the fierce weather and rolled back and forth across the deck. The men were drenched by rain and roaring waves. And then the *Rescue* started to leak! For the rest of the night and well into the following day, the crew was busy working the pumps and maintaining some semblance of order. Finally, the storm ended. Around 6 p.m., as the exhausted crew finally relaxed somewhat, the *Rescue* turned northward into the Detroit River. Two hours later, she docked at Windsor.

Meanwhile, ninety seamen and twenty marines from the *Aurora*, along with seven officers under the command of Lieutenant Fairlie, had been dispatched westward to man the *Rescue*. They reached Toronto to find that she had sailed. Captain Algernon De Horsey, who was in command of all the naval vessels on the Great Lakes, was more than a little irritated and promptly asked the governor-general for another vessel. Monck offered the *Magnet*. Built at Niagara in 1847, she had been employed as a mail vessel between Hamilton and Kingston. Although she could reach a maximum speed of fourteen and half miles per hour, her average was about twelve and a half. According to one government report, she was "the strongest Iron steamer in America & best-adapted for carrying Guns or Troops. Can carry across the Lake from 800 to 1,000 men with arms & accoutrements."[15] Nevertheless, De Horsey rejected her as unsuitable and too expensive to refit. Instead, the Royal Navy sailors were sent off to Windsor to replace the Toronto Naval Brigade, who returned home with the understanding that they would crew the *Magnet*.[16] On June 10, before the boat was fully prepared, the government cancelled its lease,[17] although the blow to the crew was softened somewhat with a letter from Lieutenant-Colonel William S. Durie to Captain McMaster, in which Durie expressed his thanks for the brigade's "efficient services . . . in discharging her cargo and getting the necessary armament on board in a very short time and in a highly creditable manner, and when relieved from the charge of the Rescue in performing similar good services when placed in charge of the steamer Magnet." Although there were also promises to bring the men's services to the attention of the governor-general and to use them again when needed, the brigade disbanded a short time later. According to a report in the *Daily Leader*, it was apparently a decision made by the men. "Ill-usage on the part of the Government is given as the cause."[18]

Hercules and *Canada* didn't fare much better than the *Magnet*. They were leased until June 24 and June 26, respectively.[19]

Some of the boats the government leased were put into

service on the St. Lawrence, such as the *St. Andrew*, which patrolled the area between Brockville and Gananoque. Many were prepared in some way for their new incarnations as naval vessels, usually with the addition of guns or metal plating. By July 17, while the British gunboats were en route to the Great Lakes from Halifax, there were five candidates under consideration for an embryonic Canadian navy: *St. Andrew*, *Royal*, *Rescue*, *Hercules* and *Michigan*, with the suggestion that at least four should be purchased outright, although there were those who argued that leasing was a more economical approach.

The leasing arrangement for the *Royal* was probably typical of those drawn up for the other vessels. She was in Montreal at the beginning of June 1866. Owned by Denis and James Gaherty of J&D Gaherty & Co., she was a relatively new 146-ton vessel. The government offered $120 Canadian per day for delivery of the vessel in perfect order, "with Boats, rope, tackle, engine, boiler and appurtenances complete." The Gahertys were required to provide fuel for the first twenty-four hours of service, plus pay the salaries of a crew consisting of a captain at $52 per month; an engineer at $40 per month; three firemen at $10 per month each; three deckhands at $9 per month each; and a pilot for the waters between Bic, Quebec, and Kingston, Ontario, at $32 per month. For replacement purposes, the *Royal* was valued at $20,000, and the lease stated that she would be returned to her owners in good condition, reasonable wear and tear excepted.[20] Aside from the initial twenty-four hours of operation, fuel to power the vessel would be paid for by the government.

In contrast, the arrangement with McCallum for use of the *Robb* was a bit more complicated. Soon after her adventure at Fort Erie, the *Robb* was fitted with boilerplate and armed with 9- and 12-pound howitzers. She patrolled the Niagara River and part of Lake Erie until June 21, when her services were no longer required. On June 25, McCallum sent his bill to the government, which included $5,000 for twenty days' rental at $250 per day, $50 for damage done by the Fenians, $20 for other damages, $75 for lumber used to house the soldiers on the boat, $40 board for eight members of the St. Catharines Garrison Battery and $10 for stationery on which he kept records and wrote his reports.[21]

Even considering that the *Robb* had been under fire, the expenses were higher than any other boat leased for a similar period and the government apparently balked at paying the full account. McCallum, however, was insistent, as a letter written on August 30 illustrates:

> . . . whatever you pay other boats has nothing to do with my claim. I did not wait to be chartered or even ask what they would pay me when I was wanted for service, but I thought that the Government would pay me the same as I could make otherways [sic] at my usual business and I do not feel disposed to take any less as settlement in full. When you speak of other boats I do not know what boats you mean or what services rendered, do you class my boat with the Hercules, the Martamora [sic], or Michigan, now, sir, I dislike to boast of what the Tug W.T. Robb done . . . as we only done our duty but the facts stands this I gave the boat when they wanted her regardless off [sic] what they would pay me and went into the fight at Fort Erie. I fed her men when they could get nothing to eat anywhere . . . and further made a hospital of my boat

and . . . was under steam night and day for twenty days and running continually and you are aware that this cannot be done without money, and since that time whenever my boat goes into Buffalo I have to keep a strong guard on her for she has been shot at twice since at Buffalo . . . I have not charged against the Government but what I can prove to be reasonable.[22]

The government eventually agreed to pay $200 per day for the lease of the *Robb*, conceding that some compensation should be made for the threats against her.[23] In all, McCallum received $4,000 but his dissatisfaction at getting less than he had counted on may have been what spurred him to keep a close eye on naval expenditures over the ensuing months and, in time, to publicly request a full accounting.

McCallum's letter of August 30 was addressed to George H. Wyatt of Toronto. "An experienced vessel-owner and ship broker," Wyatt was thirty-seven, had been involved in shipping on Canadian inland waters for at least ten years, and was "highly qualified to value and charter steamers." [24]

He seems to have been at work before July 6, 1866, the date on which the Ministry of Marine confirmed his appointment as government agent in charge of leasing and purchasing boats, as well as hiring crews. His salary was five dollars per day, plus travelling expenses.[25] Although his appointmentwasnotconfirmeduntilmorethanamonthafterthe Fenian invasion, it appears he was involved in the organization of naval defence right from the beginning, and he may well have been the same George Wyatt who sailed as quartermaster with the Toronto Naval Brigade aboard the *Rescue*.

For most of the summer and early fall of 1866, Wyatt was kept busy inspecting boats, making arrangements for their hire or purchase and overseeing any upgrades necessary to make them useful for border defence. One of the factors he had to consider in carrying out his duties was the kinds of boats the Americans had at their disposal.

A week after the *Robb*'s lease ended, Gilbert McMicken, magistrate and head of Canada's embryonic secret service the Western Frontier Constabulary, reported on armed American vessels on the Great Lakes. McMicken listed nine boats, one of which, the *Michigan*, was the navy gunboat that had patrolled the Niagara River at the time of the invasion. Her speed was not given, but she was well armed with one 64-pounder, three 32-pounders, and three 12-pounders. Six others were revenue cutters: *S.F. Chase, Commodore Perry, William Pitt Fessenden, John Sherman, Andrew Johnson* and *John A. Dix*. The *Chase* patrolled Lake Ontario; the *Perry* and *Fessenden* were on Lake Erie; and the *Sherman* was on Lake Huron, but focused mainly on the Detroit River to Saginaw. *Andrew Johnson* was on Lake Michigan from Saginaw Bay to Milwaukee, and the *Dix* was on Lake Superior. With the exception of the *Fessenden*, which was armed with two 24-pounders, the vessels each had one 30-pounder and could reach a speed of about sixteen miles per hour, which was considered quite fast.[26] The remaining two boats were *Search*, a survey vessel with a small gun whose area of patrol and speed were not given, and *Little Ada*. Based in Detroit, *Little Ada* was a steamer being converted for revenue service, so, although her speed and armaments were not listed, she probably would compare with the other six revenue cutters when refitted.

While the revenue cutters were more concerned about smugglers and poachers, there were fears that they might be commandeered by Fenians or authorized by the United

States government to attack Canada. From McMicken's point of view, their speed was worrisome (even if it may have been somewhat exaggerated); others agreed, which was why De Horsey advised Canadian authorities to continue renting the *Rescue*. The *Michigan* (not to be confused with the American gunboat *Michigan*, which patrolled the Niagara River) was also highly regard because of her suitable size and speed. As a result, George Wyatt spent much of the summer of 1866 discussing whether or not these two boats should be purchased and under what terms.

By November 1, 1867, the Canadian government would spend $126,632 on gunboats, including $70,348 for leases, $37,787.50 for outright purchases, $4,279.50 for equipment, $3,272 for repairs and $10,945 for iron-plating seven steamers — five of which had already been dismantled,[27] some within just a few weeks of being put into service. However, measures were initiated to allow the steamers to get back into action as quickly as possible if needed. When *Canada*, which was rented from June 4 to 26, 1866, was decommissioned, the iron plates installed to give her some protection from bullets, along with wooden beams used in customizing the vessel, were numbered and carefully stored so the boat could be refitted quickly and with minimal expense and effort.[28] The same procedure was used with other vessels.

The biggest challenge facing both the government and the British navy was finding suitable ships. Tugs and fishing boats might do in a pinch, but what was really needed was purpose-built boats. It was more than a matter of being able to efficiently carry out the business of defence. Employing vessels designed to meet the enemy in combat sent a clear message that the danger the Fenians posed to Canadians was being taken seriously and merited the attention of the legendary Royal Navy. Before June was out, the Canadian government and higher-ranking members of the Royal Navy were aware that purpose-built gunboats were being sent from Britain to defend the lakes. Captain De Horsey had travelled to both Fort Erie and Windsor to see for himself how vulnerable both locations were and how badly gunboats were needed. Both places had been visited by at least one of the leased vessels, and De Horsey was struck by "what confidence the presence of a Gunboat at each of those places has inspired."[29] Aside from the practical matter of providing appropriate naval defence, authorities in Canada and Britain kept a careful eye on the mood of the Canadian people.

There was no doubt that the colonies in British North America were at a crossroads. Discussions surrounding Confederation were part of the fabric of everyday life, and not everyone was completely in favour of the union. In Britain, there was a strong drive towards limiting both monetary and military support for the colonies. If Canadians wanted a form of independence, it was argued, then they should pay for it. And, through all this, there was the lure of a closer connection with the United States. The Reciprocity Treaty between the two countries had ended in 1866; to some extent, it was a victim of the friction that had erupted during the course of the American Civil War. Yet the possibility that some, or perhaps all, of the British North American colonies would merge with the United States was always in the background.

For this reason, it was with some gratification that high-placed observers were able to report on the mood of Canadians and their response to the Fenian invasion. Writing to Edward Cardwell on June 14, Lord Monck was eloquent in his praise of Canadians' loyalty to the throne, appreciation of British institutions and willingness to take both financial and physical risks to defend their way of life. Their reaction, he stressed, was particularly noteworthy because of the time of year at which the attacks took place.

Nothing comparable to a modern welfare state existed in 1860s Canada. Religious organizations provided some forms of charity for the indigent, frequently in the form of free food or shelter. Mutual benevolent organizations, often created by members of a particular trade or ethnic group, might provide some cash relief when a worker was unemployed due to accident or illness, or benefits in the case of death, but generally these were only available to organization members who had contributed to the benevolent fund. Some rudimentary services for the elderly, orphans and the physically or mentally handicapped were provided by "houses of refuge" or "county homes"—although, in some jurisdictions, those who were very old, very young or incapacitated might as easily end up in the local jail. Avoiding these grim prospects could be a significant struggle for many people, especially in the colder months. A great many Canadians were seasonally employed, in farming, fishing and water transportation. Unless a worker had saved up a bit of cash — a difficult task, given the wages at the time — the late fall through mid-spring was often a struggle for survival, a determined bid to hold on until better times rolled around. In 1866, the Fenians attacked just around the time that jobs were starting to open up again. As a result, when the call went out for militia volunteers, many of those who responded did so with the knowledge that they were putting their livelihoods in jeopardy. While there certainly would have been exceptions, many employers simply did not have the luxury, let alone the inclination, of holding a job open for a man who was off on a military assignment. Monck understood this, as his note to Cardwell made evident:

> The period of the year at which the people has been called on to make these sacrifices of time by servicing the Volunteer ranks has been the most inconvenient that could be selected, yet I have never heard a murmur from any quarter at the necessity for suspending industrial occupation involving the risk of losing a whole year's production.[30]

On the contrary, he had heard volunteers complain about being turned down when their services were offered!

In the same letter, Monck commented favourably on American efforts to stop the Fenian incursions. Apparently, Cardwell was impressed:

> Your account of the spirit which animates the Canadian people, of their appreciation of the free institutions under which they live, and of their loyalty to the Throne, is in the highest degree satisfactory. The cheerfulness with which they suspended their industrial occupations in order to serve in the ranks of the Volunteers; and the zeal which they exhibited in the service reflects the greatest credit upon them.[31]

By this time, Monck had formally requested four gunboats for service on the lakes. Although only three were assigned, it was definitely a step in the right direction. De Horsey saw value in this. But, he cautioned, "I do not think we have any vessels suitable for lake service, and building them will be a matter of time." Furthermore, the British gunboats weren't as powerful as they could be. "At Fort Erie, I doubt their being able to stem the current at the upper entrance of Niagara River, in which case if they once got in they could not easily get out again,"[32] De Horsey commented. In his opinion, the best boats available for the task at hand were the *Michigan* and *Rescue*, which, "[a]lthough not the class of vessel it would be desirable to build as Gunboats, are nevertheless very good substitutes, being fast and strongly built, and capable, particularly the *Michigan*."[33] As he wrote the letter, the boats were being clad in armour and, fearing that the owners would raise the selling price once that was done, he urged the governor-general to arrange for their immediate purchase.[34]

He was not alone in his opinion. Wyatt agreed, and so did Lieutenant Fairlie, who had taken over command of the Toronto Naval Brigade on June 10 and come to that conclusion within three weeks. In his opinion, the *Rescue* was the most suitable vessel he had encountered for service on the Great Lakes. Built in 1854, he described her as "fast, strong . . . well adapted for fighting & the officers & men are very comfortable."[35] Able to burn coal or wood (coal was preferred, as it allowed for greater speed), she would accommodate between 200 and 250 men. She drew about eight-and-a half feet, making it possible for her to navigate all canals and rivers between Quebec City and Fort William. Although the *Michigan* was newer and more widely admired for her speed, in Wyatt's opinion, navigational prowess made the *Rescue* more valuable than the *Michigan*.[36] By the beginning of July, she had been fitted with metal plating, and a powder room had been constructed. She had also been fitted with two guns at midship and another forward, which were better suited than the oversized 32-pounder that had originally been installed. As Wyatt reported, "she stood the recoil well."[37] At this point, she was being rented for $150 a day.

The *Michigan*, a "propeller boat" with one screw engine, was considerably longer at 160 feet. Measuring 26' across, she was capable of transporting up to 300 troops if required. While her hull was substantial and she could move at a rate of thirteen to fourteen miles per hour, she lacked masts, sailboats, life preservers and other equipment necessary to make her ideal for government needs. She also had the disadvantage of drawing too much water to navigate the St. Lawrence and the canals of the Province of Canada. Wyatt, among others, was in favour of purchasing her because of her speed.[38] At the beginning of July, her lease cost the government $130 per day.[39]

Based on Wyatt's information, William McDougall reported to Lord Monck on July 5 that the *Rescue* could be purchased for $22,000; the *Michigan*, for $12,000.[40] The following day, Wyatt was instructed to make an offer to the owners in writing, but, if he felt the price they asked was too high, to consider other suitable vessels. The advice was timely. On July 9, John Pridgeon, the owner of the *Michigan*, wrote to Wyatt offering to sell the boat for $25,000 — more than double the figure McDougall reported.[41]

Around the same time, Cook Brothers of Toronto offered the *Rescue* to Wyatt for $21,000, less than originally suggested.[42] A considerable amount of work had to be done to convert her for naval use, and Wyatt was not yet sure how much that would cost the government. But, he reported to McDougall, the *Rescue* was "in perfect order for work"[43] or would be once the conversion was complete. He anticipated that would be done by Wednesday, July 11, but before his letter reached McDougall, Gilbert McMicken urged that the boat be sent to Fort Erie immediately as a precaution against Fenian incursions. She left straight away, stopping en route in St. Catharines for some quick repairs.

While discussion on whether to purchase or continue to lease continued, the owner of the *Michigan* insisted he would stick to the asking price of $25,000, and McMicken personally went to see Pridgeon to attempt to change his mind. In the meantime, there were some who had serious misgivings about the suitability of both the *Michigan* and the *Rescue*. On July 9, Samuel Risley, an inspector with the board of steamboat inspection, expressed his concerns, which included a rather low opinion of the *Rescue*. "She is an old Vessel, 12 years, and if brought into action might be found pretty shaky." That did not jibe with Wyatt's assessment, but Risley could not be ignored.

Nevertheless, on July 13, Wyatt advised McDougall that, in accordance with his instructions, he was proceeding with the purchase of both vessels. That same day, George I. Cook of Toronto formally accepted the offer for the *Rescue*.[44]

The deal with the *Michigan* owner still needed to be ironed out — Pridgeon had refused McMicken's request for a lower price — but Wyatt was still optimistic about eventually closing the sale. In anticipation of that, he suggested that the name of the boat be changed. First off, it would avoid confusion with the American gunboat *Michigan*, but, beyond that, it simply wasn't politic to retain the American name. The new name choice honoured Queen Victoria's second son, the future Duke of Edinburgh, who had entered the navy as a boy. In 1866, at the age of twenty-two, he was serving as captain aboard the corvette HMS *Raccoon*.

The government's strategy was to proceed with the purchase of the vessels to avoid having to pay any additional leasing costs. It was understood, however, that outstanding amounts connected to the leasing or improvements owners had undertaken on behalf of the government would eventually be paid. But the sales could fall through if something was found seriously amiss with the boats. With that end in mind, around July 20, Wyatt went to Sarnia to inspect the *Michigan*, which had recently arrived from Goderich. But he was not the only one concerned with her condition. Three days later, steamboat inspector Samuel Risley wrote to J.G. Vansittart stating that it was entirely possible than neither of the boats was suitable for government service.[45] As late as July 27, McDougall was advising Wyatt by telegram to stop completion of the sale of the *Rescue*, if possible, until she was inspected.[46] That finally happened around the beginning of August. Although the *Michigan* needed some caulking on her decks and plank, the hull, engines and boilers were sound, and the seven-year-old vessel was not only considered "well and substantially built" but "could be made into an effective and useful gunboat."[47]

The *Rescue* was another matter. Risley claimed she had already been ruled unfit for service once and had been used only part-time as a passenger boat and for towing rafts. At this point he considered her "fairly sound and seaworthy." She might be good for another three years' service, but he still did not consider her safe as a gunboat. The boilers and the engines were partially exposed to enemy fire and might well explode during a fight, killing everyone on board. In addition, it was his opinion that "the vessel is not strong enough to carry armour plating."[48] The stark contrast between the inspector's assessment of the *Rescue* and that of both Lieutenant Fairlie and Wyatt suggests political motives were in play here. Ultimately, Risley was thwarted, and the purchase of both vessels went ahead.

That did not solve all of Wyatt's problems. Some of them were comparatively minor, such as making sure that adequate amounts of coal were available for the leased and purchased vessels, and that the coal supplies were stockpiled appropriately. Then there was the little problem with blankets. As Wyatt explained to McDougall, the supply that had been delivered were "white and best quality and could not be kept clean on a steamer" because of the ever-present coal dust. He had therefore written to Dr. Joseph Workman at the Provincial Lunatic Asylum in Toronto, offering to sell him the entire supply, but if that did not work out, he recommended that McDougall arrange for their sale at the best possible price and then their replacement with something cheaper, around $1.50 apiece. Grey was the only colour suitable for use on steamers.

A more serious problem concerned the *Royal*. The owners, possibly miffed because the boat had been seriously considered for purchase but no offer had been made, had created a huge fuss about compensation for alleged damage during the term of her lease. In retrospect, it appears they were attempting to gouge compensation from the government. The Gahertys argued that they should be compensated for the use of the vessel even after the navigation season had ended. They also would not concede that they should foot the bill for normal wear and tear to the vessel or repairs to the boiler and engines, or for a stolen boat and a coil of rope.[49] And while the matter of manpower on the three British gunboats was outside Wyatt's mandate, it was something he had to address to some extent when it came to the boats hired or purchased by the Canadian government.

Most of the crew on the Canadian vessels were British navy men, typically a sub-lieutenant, assistant surgeon, midshipman and engineer, plus thirty seamen and boys and six marines. According to Wright, "Each seaman and boy was armed with rifle, revolver, and cutlass; each marine with rifle and revolver. Also, each man was allotted 2,000 rounds of rifle ammunition and 100 rounds of pistol ammunition."[50] Augmenting their ranks, at least for a little while when the leases first went into effect, were civilian sailors. Getting the right calibre of men and keeping them proved to be a bit of a chore, although there was a flurry of applicants eager to get involved in what seemed to be the beginnings of a Canadian navy.

While most Canadians may not have been aware of the details of the government's efforts to assemble a suitable fleet of gunboats, enough information was available to the public to prompt rumours that Canada was forming her own navy, or, at the very least, hiring sailors to man the government gunboats. Predictably, a number of individuals sought employment. On July 16, 1866, nineteen-year-old R. Oliver Jr. of Guelph wrote to the provincial secretary asking if there were plans to establish a Canadian navy and requesting a commission. William McDougall responded, stating that there were no such plans.[51] On July 21, Captain Alexander Cameron wrote from the Windsor area offering to serve as master of the *Michigan*. A native of Glengarry County in eastern Ontario, he had been a master and pilot on the St. Lawrence for fifteen years and was then sailing on the St. Clair and Detroit Rivers.[52] On July 27, two MPPs, Walter McCrea and Archibald Allan, recommended Robert McCorquodale of Chatham as a pilot for one of the gunboats on the upper lakes. Accompanying the letter was a testimonial to McCorquodale's experience and trustworthiness. He had been sailing on the lakes since boyhood and was "a good practical sailor and an efficient pilot." Dated July 5, the testimonial was signed by twenty-three people.[53] McDougall replied diplomatically, saying that if a pilot was required he would be happy to consider McCorquodale.[54] With two elected representatives supporting McCorquodale, McDougall had to tread carefully, but he was not always so tactful. McDougall replied tersely to Cameron's request, stating, "I have no knowledge of there being a vacancy in the command of that steamer."[55]

The applicants may not have been so eager to work on the gunboats had they been aware of some of the problems encountered by those who were hired. Low wages and delayed payments were common problems faced by sailors, even when the security of the country was in jeopardy. In late July 1866, it was learned that the crew of the *Michigan* had not been paid for forty-five days. Reiterating his own telegram and McMicken's concerns about the impact of this, Wyatt advised McDougall, "Some of the crew being Americans are making trouble and speaking very disrespectfully of the Government in Detroit and elsewhere for not paying them. Such men should be paid up and kicked off as soon as possible [for] setting a bad example to the sailors."[56]

Wyatt asked for authorization to pay all "urgent demands" of the crew.[57] Under normal conditions, desertions were frequent enough among both merchant seamen and sailors of the Royal Navy. The last thing needed when an invasion threatened was the difficulty of dealing with a disgruntled crew.

On July 28, just four days after authorizing Wyatt to pay the *Michigan* crew, McDougall instructed him to reduce the crew sizes as soon as the purchases of the *Michigan* and *Rescue* were completed. Wyatt was also asked to create a nominal crew list, "shewing the duty of every officer and man, and stating those who might, in your opinion, be dispensed with." At the same time, knowing how politically loaded the situation of naval defense was, McDougall warned Wyatt to make sure to get the opinion of the Royal Navy officers in command of the vessels before submitting his recommendation.[58]

On August 24, Wyatt submitted a list which included a pilot for the lakes at $60 per month; a river pilot at $50; a first engineer at $50; second engineer at $25; two firemen to tend the fires essential to steam operation, one at $20, one at $16; and a cook at $20.

Despite Wyatt's familiarity with working conditions on the lakes, the wages really weren't adequate. On October 6, 1866, as the end of the navigational season neared, James Rice, first engineer on *Prince Alfred* wrote to George Wyatt, complaining that the $25-per-month salary paid to the second engineer was too low and the man had announced his decision to leave. "I am sure I cannot get any man that knows any thing about an Engine for any such a figure."[59] Rice also complained about his own wages, which were $50 per month. Four days later, Lieutenant J. Maxwell Heron, commander of the *Prince Alfred*, added his views on the matter. In his opinion, both engineers were "first rate men" but the second engineer was leaving unless he received a ten-dollar increase:

> I think it will be a great pity to lose so good a man . . . Between them they have improved the working of the engine greatly & put it to rights for it was . . . going to the dogs . . .[60]

Wyatt was pretty much in agreement. At the beginning of February 1867, he urged McDougall to hire engineers as soon as possible, stressing that the best men were usually employed by the end of February and the longer the delay, the lower the chance of finding top-rate men. And it wasn't just a matter of finding someone to occupy the position. As far as Wyatt was concerned, much of the repairs that had to be done to the gunboats' engines came about as a direct result of employing inadequately qualified engineers.[61]

Wyatt's activities took up an incredible amount of time and energy and were vital to the creation of a first line of defence against a Fenian naval attack. But, right from the first, in spite of the quick action of the Dunnville and Toronto naval brigades, the general public was far more interested in a British naval presence, specifically the gunboats promised for the Great Lakes. While George Wyatt hustled back and forth from one port to another via boat or rail, scribbling notes and letters and telegrams as he went, most citizens were avidly reading about the progress of the *Britomart*, *Cherub* and *Heron* as they made their way westward from Halifax.

CHAPTER 5
The Gunboats Arrive

In *The Navy in Transition*, historian Michael Lewis discusses the role of the Royal Navy and "gunboat diplomacy" during the 19th century. According to his analysis, after the Battle of Trafalgar in 1805, the Royal Navy underwent a metamorphosis, changing from a "national warrior" whose main interests were those of Britain, into an "international policeman, acting dispassionately in the interest of all sea-users." Lewis, whose book was published during the Second World War, tended to be rather naïve and jingoistic in his analysis, since Britain had much to gain in its role as international policeman.[1] However, he was generally correct in his conclusion that the Royal Navy was "the prime instrument" responsible for *Pax Britannica*, the long period of comparative peace that characterized the 19th century.[2]

In another work, Lewis presents the navy as the "policeman of the seas." While a bit whimsical, it illustrates how effective the mere presence of the right authority figure could be. He characterized a policeman as a large, good-natured fellow who spent more time preventing problems that taking wrong-doers into custody. The role of the policeman, Lewis explains, is to guide people to appropriate action, rather than to use arms or force. Simply by being present, he made the community a safer place for everyone, and this, Lewis argues, is precisely what the Royal Navy also did.

To substantiate his argument, Lewis offers an account of gunboat diplomacy. On May 11, 1860, during the unification of Italy, Garibaldi's forces attempted a landing in Sicily. One of the ships, the *Lombardo*, ran aground and made an easy target for three Neapolitan warships that subsequently arrived. While perfectly capable of destroying the *Lombardo*, the Neapolitans hesitated, knowing two British ships, the *Intrepid* and *Argus*, were less than a mile away. In addition, the commander of the Neapolitan ships was half-British and, rather than engage in hostilities, decided to confer with one of the British captains. The latter delayed the rendezvous long enough to allow Garibaldi's troops to land safely.[3] Although Lewis's description is a little fanciful and ethnocentric — was the ancestry of the Neapolitan commander really a factor? — this story and other, similar tales would have no doubt been familiar to newspaper readers all over the British Empire, including Canadians. It is hardly surprising that the government and the public regarded gunboats as an effective solution to the perceived Fenian threat.

British North Americans may not have been familiar with the term *gunboat diplomacy*, but it seems they had some appreciation of its impact, judging by the reaction to the arrival of the three British gunboats in the summer of 1866. As usual, Halifax was quite a sight that June. The bustling seaport welcomed merchant vessels of every description, powered by steam and sail, as well as vessels of the Royal Navy, which made the seaport central to the North American and West Indies Squadron. According to the *Grand River Sachem*, there were at least thirteen British men-of-war in the harbour. On almost any day, the waters around Halifax were crowded to overflowing, crammed with battleships, barges, clippers, sloops — vessels of nearly every size from ports all over the world. Of these, three British gunboats, *Britomart, Cherub* and *Heron*, were of particular interest to the people of the Province of Canada, as the ships prepared to make their way westward to protect the Great Lakes from further Fenian invasions.

The boats chosen for duty in Canadian waters belonged to the Britomart[4] class, the only suitable vessels that could navigate the shallow canals joining the St. Lawrence and the Great Lakes. They were designed as an improvement on the Dapper class, which had been employed in the shallow waters of the Baltic and Black Seas during the Crimean War. The Britomart class was also the last of British naval ships designed with wooden hulls. Like most naval vessels of the period, the gunboats could be powered by either steam or sail. The single-screw propeller could be raised to increase sailing speed when the boats relied on the wind. *Britomart* and the others of her class were three-masted, barquentine-rigged vessels. The *Britomart* was armed with two 68-pounder smooth bore muzzle loading cannons when she was launched in May 1860, but the *Heron*, launched two months later, had two 112-pounder Armstrong guns and the *Cherub*, launched March 1865, had 68-pounder rifled muzzle-loaders.

Named for an ancient Cretan goddess, the patron of fishermen, hunters and sailors, twenty Britomart-class vessels were planned (and sixteen built) during the 1860s. The *Britomart*, which gave her name to the class, was the first. She had a 105'8" keel, was 22'1" across the beam, weighed 270 tons, and was equipped with a two-cylinder reciprocating sixty-horsepower steam engine. A smokestack mounted on hinges was just forward of midships. She drew just eight feet of water and could reach a speed of nine knots. *Britomart* and her sister ships could carry a crew of approximately forty officers and ratings — sailors on warships.[5]

She was commanded by Lieutenant Alington, who had taken over from Basil E. Cochrane on March 31. The crew consisted of thirty-nine men, including six officers (instead of the usual seven), six petty officers, nineteen seamen, a steward, a cook, a cabin boy and five marines.[6] The other two gunboats, with similar-sized crews, were the *Cherub* (105'7" keel, 22'9" beam, 268 tons), commanded by Lieutenant Spencer Robert Huntley, and *Heron* (105'6"keel, 22'1" beam, 270 tons), commanded by Henry Frederick Stephenson.

The three gunboats commenced the 1866 season departing England at the end of April and the beginning of May. They headed first for Madeira, where they rendezvoused in Funchal Bay. Before reaching their destination, Alington had found it necessary to jettison 161 pounds of beef found "unfit for food," tossing it overboard on May 2. Meanwhile, on the *Cherub*, Lieutenant Huntley had far more serious problems to contend with. On May 6, en route to Madeira, a doctor was called aboard from a nearby ship, HMS *Pallas*, to care for the *Cherub*'s boatswain, Shadrack Gordon. The unfortunate man died a short time later and, at 5:15 that evening, wrapped in a sheet and hammock, his body was "committed to the deep."[7]

After a brief pause in Madeira, the *Heron* and *Britomart* set out for Bermuda on May 9, steaming out of Funchal Bay together before separating. It is not clear exactly when *Cherub* left, but she was bound for Bermuda by May 18. On June 5, the *Heron* and *Britomart* rendezvoused briefly in Bermuda before heading for Halifax on June 7. Four days out, the *Britomart* ran into a severe storm, which caused a little bit of damage to the ship and resulted in the loss of some supplies: seventy-five pounds of biscuits and forty pounds of raisins were soaked; eleven pounds of beef, nineteen pounds of pork, and thirty pounds of suet were washed overboard. But there was still plenty of food left, and the journey continued northward without incident. *Britomart* reached Halifax on June 15; *Heron* arrived two days later. *Cherub*, which had reached Bermuda June 16, took a little longer, finally getting to Halifax on June 22. Soon afterward, there were indications of the discipline problems that would plague the vessel for months to come, as the ship's log book states that at 6:30 on the morning of June 25, Joseph Parker was punished with forty-eight lashes.

Britomart, *Heron* and *Cherub* received a supply of guns from a larger ship, the *Barracouta*, carried out minor repairs and took on supplies. On July 4, as a tribute to American Independence Day, the boats were decked out in flags, much as *Britomart* and *Heron* had been on June 20, in honour of the anniversary of Queen Victoria's ascension to the throne.

On July 7, the *Britomart*, *Heron* and *Cherub* prepared to leave Halifax. Because there was a heavy fog, three larger ships, the *Wolverene*, *Barracouta* and *Favourite*, towed them. As they were leaving, Henry Chambers, boatswain's mate aboard *Britomart*, became sick for the second time since arriving in Halifax. Lieutenant Alington hailed the *Wolverene*, asking for a doctor to be sent aboard. The next day, with Chambers presumably recovered, the ships left the gunboats. The trio made their way up the St. Lawrence, and by July 16 were taking on coal in Quebec harbour. On July 17, Captain De Horsey of the HMS *Aurora* inspected the gunboats prior to their departure for Montreal.

De Horsey, thirty-nine, was in charge of all British vessels on the Great Lakes. The grandson of the first Earl of Stradbroke and son-in-law of Admiral Andrew Drew, he was a rather fussy character who was a stickler for protocol and seemed to take offence easily. This may have been a result of personal circumstances more than anything else, as his sister Adeline was notorious for her affair with the Earl of Cardigan, who had led the famous Charge of the Light Brigade in 1854. Their involvement while the Earl's second wife was still alive was public knowledge, and although Adeline and her lover married in 1858, she was not welcome in polite society.

It would be an exaggeration to suggest that everyone in the navy knew the details of De Horsey's sister's life. But enough people certainly would have been aware of some of the scandal, notably young, up-and-coming officers such as the commanders Alington, Huntley and Stephenson on the gunboats.

Alington's family had aristocratic connections. William Alington was created Baron Alington by Charles II. The title became extinct following the death of Hildebrand, second Lord Alington in 1692, but the family line continued and Arthur Alington was born at Swinhope Hall, a graceful Georgian house in Lincolnshire, on October 10, 1839.

The family had lived in the area since the early 17th century and the house dated from the late 1770s.

Young Arthur entered the navy as a cadet at the age of fourteen and acquitted himself well. In 1861, just five days after transferring to *Rinaldo*, he saved someone from drowning and was commended for gallantry by his commander. It was also on board the *Rinaldo* that he received some important first-hand experience in international diplomacy because of the *Trent* affair. The *Rinaldo* was chosen to transport Slidell and Mason, the Confederate diplomats captured by the Union, after their release from custody. Their transfer, which had to be handled very diplomatically, would certainly have impressed the twenty-two-year-old first lieutenant.

The *Britomart* was Alington's first command, just as the *Cherub* was the first command for Huntley, twenty-five. Huntley had an interesting Canadian connection — his father, Sir Henry Vere Huntley, was a naval officer and colonial administrator who had served as lieutenant governor of Prince Edward Island from 1841 to 1847.

Stephenson was also enjoying his first independent command, although he had a somewhat longer naval career than his two counterparts. His father was the Duke of Norfolk and his maternal grandfather was the fourth Earl of Albermarle, one of whose sons was the Honourable Henry Keppell, a noted naval officer. At the age of nine, Stephenson was sent to sea with his uncle and had spent some time in the Far East before his appointment to the *Heron*.

The similar backgrounds shared by the young commanders was a crucial component of gunboat diplomacy. They were very much part of the British establishment, with family roots that went deep into British soil, and their upbringing had given them some preparation for dealing with individuals who wielded a certain amount of power, such as representatives of colonial governments. The social skills they typically were expected to develop would serve them well in their careers.

On July 19, the three gunboats set out from Quebec together, but *Heron* ran into problems and *Britomart* towed her to Sorel. Repairs were quickly carried out, enabling the *Heron* to join *Britomart* and *Cherub* just a few hours after they reached Montreal on July 21. The next few days were spent in minor repairs and maintenance, taking on more supplies and carrying out routine duties. The three ships departed for Canada West on August 1.

Although local pilots had been taken aboard, *Britomart* ran into trouble fifteen minutes after entering the Lachine Canal at 4:30 a.m. on August 3. Steam pressure suddenly dropped, and the boat drifted into the dam. A rope was connected to *Heron*, but when the screw engine was started up, it "struck a submerged pile, which bent the blades."[8]

The *Britomart* limped through the canal, after which the *Heron* took her in tow. Next morning, she continued upstream but stopped running the engine after a couple of hours, "as the screw showed signs of being out of its place." At noon, a "water telescope" was used to examine the machinery. There was enough damage to warrant her being towed by the *Cherub* during the next part of the journey.

Meanwhile, newspapers in Canada West assiduously reported the progress of the gunboats. On July 18, the *British Daily Whig* reprinted an item from the *Quebec News*, announcing the arrival of the three gunboats in Quebec harbour, naming their commanders and noting the boats were "intended for the upper lakes." Like many other newspapers, the *Whig* misspelled *Britomart*. (*Brittomart* was the most common misspelling.)[9]

Three days later, the *Whig* added more details about the gunboats: "They are bound for the upper lakes. They are armed with powerful Armstrong guns, and have an exceedingly rakish, saucy appearance."[10]

On July 26, when the *Whig* reported the boats reaching Montreal, the newspaper included a brief description of them, noting that each had two Armstrong guns.[11] Other newspapers provided similar coverage, seemingly in an effort to assure Canadians that the British gunboats were indeed on the way to provide a visible, potent presence on the Great Lakes. And now and then they added a bit of information about the reaction of Americans. "One of the gunboats, at Prescott, C.W., hoisted the American flag on the 4th of July. The people of Ogdensburgh, immediately opposite, kindly acknowledged the compliment by hoisting the Fenian flag on one of their public buildings."[12]

Along with keeping fear of the Fenians alive, newspapers focused on naval defences. Various reports in July and August provided some information on the acquisition of Canadian gunboats and the progress of the British gunboats as they travelled to the Great Lakes. Some newspapers also tried to quell rumours that the lakes were not well defended and to reassure the populace. Typical was one report that appeared in Toronto's *Daily Leader* in mid-August and was then reprinted in the *London Free Press*:

Some persons are very industrious in circulating stories about the defenceless conditions of the lakes, which have no sort of truth in them. When we remember that at the time of the last Fenian raid there was not a gunboat on the lakes, it is a matter for congratulations as well as surprise that we have now seven boats of this character upon these waters.[13]

Repeatedly, newspaper reports focused on the gunboats' armament and the speed they could attain. However, the reports were usually careful not to discuss the speed capability of the American revenue cutters, which in most cases surpassed that of British and Canadian vessels.

As the gunboats made their way along the St. Lawrence and into the Great Lakes, the residents of various towns turned out in large numbers to welcome them. The *Heron* and *Cherub* reached Kingston harbour on the night of August 6–7, 1866. The following morning, "no little excitement was got up in consequence, and the docks were lined with groups of citizens anxious to get a sight of the welcome visitors."[14] Initially, few visitors were permitted on board, but that did not dampen Kingstonians' enthusiasm one bit. The newspaper reported on the arrival of the crippled *Britomart* and attempts at repairing her broken propeller. Kingston was well equipped to handle ship repairs, but in order to get the *Britomart* out of the water via the marine railway, it would have been necessary to remove at least one of her guns, and this Lieutenant Alington refused to do. Consequently, the *Cherub* towed her across Lake Ontario to Shickluna's drydock in Port Dalhousie, near St. Catharines.[15]

However, the *Heron* lingered in Kingston, much to the delight of the local populace. On Thursday, August 9, the boat's officers were invited to dine at the mess of the Royal Canadian Rifles.[16] On August 10, a group of Good Templars, a Kingston-area temperance organization, boarded a steamer for a picnic excursion, along with a number of soldiers. As the steamer passed the *Heron* in the harbour, the gunboat was greeted with "three British cheers."[17]

That weekend, the gunboat was decorated with flags and bunting and opened to visitors. Hundreds of people took advantage of the chance for a guided tour "and were treated with that polite attention which can only be received from a genuine salt water Jack Tar on the deck of his favorite craft."[18]

The sailors answered visitors' questions, explaining every detail of the vessel's operation, especially her armaments. "What excited most attention was the Armstrong guns and the 100 pound shot intended to be used by the largest Armstrong in case it should become necessary for them to give the 'liberators of Ireland' a taste of their quality in the event of another Fenian raid . . . "[19]

Similar scenes were repeated in almost every harbour the gunboats visited. Meanwhile, there was speculation as to where the gunboats would be stationed. From time to time, different reports appeared, some of which seemed more the product of wishful thinking than responsible fact-gathering. On August 15, the *Grand River Sachem* of Caledonia reprinted a report from a Kingston newspaper announcing that the *Heron* would patrol the St. Lawrence River between Prescott and Kingston until the end of navigation.[20]

The very next day, the *St. Catharines Constitutional* claimed she would be on Lake Ontario while the *Britomart* and *Cherub* had been ordered to Lake Erie "to rove about hunting for Fenians."[21] A report in a Hamilton newspaper that also appeared on August 16 claimed the *Heron* would be stationed at Port Dalhousie "for the present."[22] And, on August 18, the *London Free Press* stated that the *Cherub*, which had reached Port Stanley, would likely stay there to guard the north shore of Lake Erie. "She will take occasional cruises up and down the lake, and be on the alert to spoil any 'little game' the Fenians may have on hand."[23]

But eventually their deployment was settled: *Heron* would go to Toronto, the capital of Canada West (soon to be Ontario), and patrol Lake Ontario. *Cherub* was destined for Lake Huron, to be based in Goderich harbour, but to patrol at least as far as Lake St. Clair. Meanwhile, *Britomart* was bound for Lake Erie. She would be stationed in Dunnville, a few miles up the Grand River.

In the long run, the specific station did not matter so much to Canadians as the fact that the gunboats had arrived and were ready to take on the Fenians. Residents of Hamilton were thrilled by the *Heron*'s visit, and especially by her armaments. Starting in the 1860s, the British navy relied on a new kind of gun for naval defence. William G. Armstrong was the inventor and had been working on the weapon that would bear his name since 1855. Accuracy had long been a problem with guns, but improvements were being introduced. One was rifling, in which grooves cut into the interior of a gun force the projectile to spin.

Armstrong also used a system involving a central metal tube, initially made of cast iron and later of steel. Wrought-iron coils were added to keep the tube under a certain amount of pressure. This, along with rifling, reduced the random movement of the projectile, increasing accuracy.

Armstrong started out with smaller guns, but at the insistence of the admiralty eventually applied his developments to bigger weapons. At first, breech loaders, where the missile was loaded from the back of the gun, were favoured, but an admiralty study concluded they were more difficult to operate quickly unless the gun crew was very well trained, and after 1865 muzzle loaders were preferred.[24]

In general, Armstrong and his guns were regarded with unbelievable respect, so much so that when the British government purchased his patents, they reimbursed him for all expenses incurred in developing the guns.[25]

Put into action in various conflicts, including the Second Opium War (1856–60), Armstrong guns became well known for their accuracy and efficiency. There was another bonus as well: They tended to be safer than their predecessors, which had a habit of exploding, killing the sailors that manned them. Given the obsession with progress and technological improvement that was the hallmark of the Victorian age, it was no surprise that newspapers frequently mentioned the presence of Armstrong guns on the *Britomart*, *Cherub* and *Heron*. In August 1867, for example, Canadians took particular delight in reading a report reprinted from the *New York Tribune*, which declared that the American Rodman gun could not compare to the Armstrong in latest trials.[26] In Port Dalhousie, a newspaper report reassured readers that the Armstrong guns on board the *Heron* and *Britomart* were so accurate that they could hit an eight-foot square target at three miles.[27] Such reports no doubt added to Canadians' feelings of security.

Also augmenting that feeling of security was a determined effort on the part of the three gunboats to visit as many places as possible once they reached the Great Lakes. De Horsey had commented on the positive impact the gunboats' arrival had in various ports. It was also crucial that the Fenians be made to feel the gunboats were likely to show up anywhere, anytime, ready to take on troublemakers. One of the first things *Britomart* did after reaching Lake Erie was to spend about a week at Port Stanley, where a contingent of Royal Artillery was also camped out. The *London Free Press* commented that the presence of both would "tend to render that ancient and pretty locality unusually jolly."[28] Although the *Britomart* returned to Port Colborne and Dunnville briefly, on September 5 she was back in Port Stanley for a few more days, before going on to Amherstburg, spending a little while there and then heading for Port Dover. She made two more trips to Port Stanley and one more to Amherstburg before navigation ended for the season. Similarly, *Cherub* called at Collingwood, Owen Sound, Kincardine and Sarnia in between periods of time in Goderich and a four-day cruise along Lake Huron. Meanwhile, the *Heron* sailed east from Toronto, visiting Kingston, Ogdensburg and Cobourg, before heading west to Niagara-on-the Lake, Queenston and Port Dalhousie, then heading for Hamilton.

Sometimes the boats stayed in harbour for just a day or two, sometimes for a week or more, in which case they were often open to visitors while, at the same time, attempting to carry on regular duties. Frequently, the men's duties included various drills with cutlasses, rifles, pistols or the big guns. While the noise might have been disturbing to some, the presence of the armed sailors and their activities was also reassuring. Canadians could see for themselves that the defenders had not only arrived, they also were making their presence felt. They were up to the challenge of meeting invaders, as an account of the *Heron*'s August visit to Hamilton makes clear.

The *Heron* travelled from Port Dalhousie, reaching Burlington Bay early the morning of Friday, August 17. News quickly spread, and in very short order, the gunboat was surrounded by a variety of small craft. Those who cared to were able to tour the *Heron*, "courteously shown about" by "Her Majesty's Jack tars." The reporter commented on her "salty" appearance, "barque rigged and copper sheathed," as well as her guns and crew.

In the afternoon, Mayor Charles Magill boarded the ship to pay his respects to Lieutenant Stephenson and verified that the gunboat would be in dock for at least another day. At 10 the next morning, he called a meeting of the city council, received its approval for a reception, then drove with members of council to the dock to pick up the *Heron*'s officers and whisk them off to the Royal Hotel where a luncheon awaited them. Toasts and speeches followed with Mayor Magill expressing the standard sentiments:

> We, the Mayor and corporation of the city of Hamilton, hail with great pleasure the arrival of gunboats in our inland waters . . . Though far removed from the heart of the empire of which we form a part, we feel conscious that we are not so far away as to be placed outside the bounds of its protection, and that its powerful aid is as vigorous to defend us in the valley of the St. Lawrence and the shores of Lake Ontario as if we were but a day's arrival from London. The arrival of your gunboat in our waters is an earnest of the sincerity of the British statesmen who said advisedly that the whole power of the empire would be made available for our defence.[29]

Lieutenant Stephenson, who had probably heard nearly identical speeches at every reception from Halifax to Hamilton, responded briefly, paying tribute to the "uniform hospitality" he and his crew had received in Canada and pledging "their readiness to do all in their power to defend the country from any attack that might be made upon it."[30] After an hour of toasts and singing, everyone piled into carriages and went to the top of the Niagara Escarpment for a view of the city and bay from Mountain View Hotel, then returned to the harbour for a quick sail. Once they were far enough from shore, the "bold and sturdy" gunnery crew wheeled out the 112-pounder Armstrong gun and demonstrated its power for the city council, some of whom were startled by the loudness of the explosion.

When the gunner playfully waved the lanyard attached to the gun in the direction of city council, silently indicating anyone who wanted to could fire it with a little tug, a number of the councillors decided discretion was the better part of valour and "retired to remote quarters of the ship." Then the *Heron* turned back towards the Desjardins Canal and fired a Congreve rocket. "[T]he peculiar and somewhat terrible fizzle which attended its ascent again severely shocked the nerves of novices in the art of war, and imparted a momentary impression that something had blown up."[31]

A few more shots were fired before the gunboat returned to the McNab Street wharf. As the city dignitaries drove away, the sailors climbed into the rigging and "hearty cheers were given for the Mayor and Corporation, and the people of Hamilton."[32]

It was an impressive display, one carefully calculated to reassure some of the most influential men in the Hamilton area that, despite the alarming reports of Fenian activity and inadequate defences, measures had been taken to protect Canadians.

A month later, the *Heron* went through a very similar exercise in Picton. Shortly after arriving early on September 18, her crew was taken under the wing of the mayor, members of the town council and officers of the 16th Battalion for a tour of the town's attractions and a sumptuous dinner at the North American Hotel. As usual, the boat was also open for visits by the general public.[33]

One reporter who visited the *Britomart* in Dunnville commented, "We have been favored with a visit by this British gunboat in our river. On going on board and viewing such implements of destruction, we wonder how the Fenians will cross the water and this gunboat too. Perhaps they will seek their own destruction."[34]

Possibly other observers who had seen the gunboats in action along Lakes Ontario, Erie and Huron had similar thoughts and, for a little while at least, discovered some renewed sense of security.

CHAPTER 6
Jolly Jack Tar

If newspaper evidence is to be believed, Canadians were caught up in a love affair with British sailors during the late summer of 1866. When the *Heron* reached Kingston on August 7, she attracted incredible attention. At times when she was in harbour, as many as forty smaller boats surrounded her on their way back and forth between the gunboat and the shore, and "[i]ndustrious boys having an eye to the main chance made a good day's work of it in conveying passengers to and fro."[1]

Most visitors came away impressed with the gunboat, the weapons, the officers and the crew. "The 'Jolly Tars' were very courteous and obliging," reported the *Daily News*, and "went a good ways to entertain their visitors, who were generally well pleased with the appearance of the vessel and the discipline and regularity that prevailed on board."[2]

Kingston was arguably the most important port on the Great Lakes, so something of a pro-naval bias might have existed, except that people's reactions in other communities were more or less the same. It did not matter whether the gunboat in question was the *Heron*, *Cherub* or *Britomart*. In Owen Sound, most of the townsfolk toured the *Cherub* and spoke highly of the "courteous treatment on board."[3] The *St. Catharines Constitutional* described the "jolly tars" of both the *Cherub* and *Britomart* as "fine dashing young fellows,"[4] and when the crew of the *Heron* marched to morning service at Toronto's St. James Cathedral on Sunday, August 19, the *Daily Leader* reported that "the jolly tars present a fine appearance."[5] Local residents seem to have taken every opportunity available to interact with the sailors, if only to acknowledge their presence through admiring glances on the city's streets.

Occasionally a little humour crept into the reports, as though the reporter (or maybe the sailors) were finding all the hero worship a little tedious. In Port Dalhousie, locals often visited the dock around meal time

> to see the brave tars eat, and at first expressed some surprise that they performed this operation just about the same as other people, bending their elbows and opening their mouths in unison and quitting with a satisfied air when the "inner man" was full. They had heard so much of the British tar, of his prowess, his tricks, and his jollity, that they thought he was different from the rest of mankind.[6]

If there was also hint of sarcasm in that report, it is understandable. The Canadian public had cast the gunboat crews as bona fide heroes and seemingly lapped up every reference that reinforced this view, even though there was a longstanding tradition of regarding sailors — especially sailors in port — as something far less than heroic. The repeated description of the sailors as "jolly" hints at this, as "jolly" was also a euphemism for "drunken" and prior to 1600 had also meant "youthfully exuberant" or "lustful."[7] Although public opinion was changing, for many decades sailors had been looked upon as troublemakers, at least when it came to most of their encounters with landlubbers. They might be brave and capable in the face of howling ocean storms. They might be courageous and self-sacrificing in battles to defend Britain and her colonies. But once they were ashore, they presented all kinds of problems for sedentary, law-abiding citizens.

As Judith Fingard explains in her study of 19th-century merchant sailors in the Maritimes, sailors, like soldiers and itinerant labourers, had their own culture and traditions, which did not necessarily mesh well with those of ordinary townsfolk. And, because they were transient, it was far easier for them to create trouble — anything from brawling and public drunkenness to seduction, robbery or murder — and be long gone before the authorities could attempt to punish them. Most of the time, there was no one left to vouch for them in their absence, and this lack of strong connections in the community helped raise the level of suspicion directed towards sailors.

There was also a perception that sailors were a peculiarly rowdy lot. Many of the crimes that came to the public's attention involved sailors attacking, robbing or otherwise harming other sailors. Often enough, the victim was or had been the perpetrator's superior aboard ship. This is easily explained because of the rigid discipline that prevailed on most ships, which was necessary for the smooth operation of the vessel and the survival of her crew.

Opportunities to redress real or perceived wrongs were few and far between aboard ship, but this changed once ashore, allowing, for instance, a sailor to retaliate for weeks of abuse with his fists. For sailors of the Royal Navy, this might not have been possible when dealing with overbearing superiors, even when ashore, but it certainly allowed an opportunity to settle a score with peers.

And, of course, alcohol was also involved in many instances when trouble erupted. On board, sailors were subject to naval discipline twenty-four hours a day, seven days a week. On leave, all the stops were out. Sometimes, the result wasn't much more serious than stupid behaviour. But, often enough, excessive drinking led to violence, which sometimes proved lethal. Other sailors were far more likely to be the target of this violence, but ordinary citizens fell victim frequently enough to add to sailors' reputation for dangerousness, or, at the very least, recklessness.

There was a certain tragic romanticism to life at sea, the constant battle against elemental forces of nature and the drama inherent in exotic locales, which provoked widespread admiration of seafaring men. On shore, however, these factors worked against the sailors to a certain extent. Having experienced adventures and challenges few other citizens encountered, sailors might find it more difficult to build relationships while ashore. To some extent, they were perpetual misfits, rather than once or future heroes. If an old salt died in poverty in a strange port, it might just as easily be chalked up to his own improvidence and wandering ways. The same applied if he fell ill far from home among strangers, since respectable people were expected to have forged strong bonds within the community. And there was not much more sympathy for accidental death, although, to be fair, sailors were not the only men whose jobs entailed serious hazards.

Yet, notwithstanding all this, the sailors who reached the Great Lakes on *Britomart*, *Cherub* and *Heron* were welcomed warmly. For one thing, they represented the best line of defence against the Fenians, who, in the public imagination, were far more terrifying than the worst "jolly tar" on a drunken spree. But it was also the result of revolutionary changes taking place within the Royal Navy in the mid-19th century. Harsh discipline, often administered arbitrarily, difficult working and living conditions and poor food were some of the major problems British sailors faced in the first half of the 19th century. In the 1840s, campaigns to improve working conditions for sailors led to the professionalization of the Royal Navy. Two significant pieces of legislation were the *Merchant Shipping Acts* of 1850 and 1854, which made shipboard conditions safer and more sanitary. A general increase in naval wages and other financial improvements also made a naval career more attractive. Around 1853, naval wages went up, and sailors who contributed twenty years of service after the age of eighteen became eligible for pensions.[8] Around the same period, changes were made in the way in which sailors received their wages. Up to that time, payment was doled out at the end of a voyage or contracted term of service, which meant that any family left behind had to survive on savings or other income for long periods of time, and the sailor himself was chronically short of funds. In the 1850s, monthly payments were introduced, and they were disbursed directly to the sailors wherever they happened to be at the time.[9] In 1862, naval wages were raised again.[10]

In addition, various incentives implemented allowed sailors to gradually rise through the ranks, increasing their rate of pay as they went. There were also incentives that encouraged men to rejoin once their term of service was over. Now sailors were better able to predict how much they were likely to earn and when it would reach their pockets, as well as their chances for promotion and increased remuneration. One of the results was that, by mid-century, joining the navy was a much more professional endeavour, rather than something a fellow more or less drifted into. By 1856, nearly ninety per cent of the ratings — sailors on warships — were in for the long haul, and many of them had deliberately chosen the sea as a career.[11]

All these changes, plus the reduction or abolition of severe punishments, altered shipboard culture. As historian Michael Lewis observed, "the tough, uncouth seaman" was replaced by "a professional class of public servants — that blue jacket, in fact, who was to become the idol of late-Victorian England, the hero of the cigarette packet, the music hall and the popular song."[12] The welcome given to the sailors who manned the gunboats in Canada West suggests that by 1866, the heroic blue jacket was already entrenched in the collective consciousness of Britons throughout the empire.

In the early 19th century, only officers wore uniforms; the ratings either wore whatever they chose or slops, clothing readily available from ship's stores.[13] By 1857, a uniform had begun to develop, one that made sailors readily identifiable and instilled a certain pride in the wearer. It included a blue jumper worn over blue trousers; a lighter blue collar with three thin, white tapes sewn on it; a pea jacket; a black silk neckerchief; and a straw or cloth hat trimmed with ribbons, often inscribed with the name of the ship on which the sailor was serving.[14]

Other changes targeted the sailors' diet. Around the late 1840s, meals aboard ship usually consisted of "bread, beef and beer;"[15] grog — watered rum — was also provided. By the early 1860s, sailors had a choice of cocoa, tea, coffee and water. Biscuits, which had often been riddled with worms in the past, were fresher and more palatable. Depending on the location, the sailors' diet might also include rice, flour, barley or peas, as well as beef or pork, vegetables and possibly tinned potatoes. There were also little luxuries, including mustard, pepper, currants, raisins and sugar.[16] The *Britomart*'s log for June 9, 1866, lists biscuits, raisins, beef, pork and suet. Based on the boat's log, it appears fresh food, specifically meat, vegetables and soft bread, was delivered daily whenever the boats were in port.

***

While the men aboard the British gunboats might have been regarded as a homogeneous lot by outside observers, considerable differences emerge when naval records are examined. Detailed personnel records are available for 126 men who served aboard the *Britomart*, *Cherub* or *Heron* in Canadian waters.[17] Although there are some gaps in the records, typically they included the sailor's name, rank, date of birth, place of origin, religion, marital status, trade (if any), height and a brief physical description that usually included colour of hair and eyes and sometimes mentioned distinguishing features. The majority of crew members (ninety) came from England, with nearly every English county represented. Forty-two per cent of these men came from Devonshire and Cornwall, areas with a strong seafaring tradition, with twenty-nine men coming from Devonshire and nine from

Cornwall. On both the *Britomart* and *Heron*, these groups accounted for more than half the crewmen whose origins were known: sixteen (53.3 per cent) in the case of the *Britomart*, and seventeen (56.7 per cent) in the case of the *Heron*. However, these two counties were dramatically under-represented on the *Cherub*, with only three men coming from Devonshire and two from Cornwall, for a combined total of 16.7 per cent, or less than a third of those aboard the other two gunboats. This situation may have had profound impact on discipline aboard the *Cherub*, as we shall see.

In addition to English crew members, there was a sprinkling of Scots and Irish, as well as two sailors from Canada West (Toronto and Kingston), and two black sailors — one from Kingston, Jamaica, and the other from Antigua. Not surprisingly, given their nationalities, forty-three of the fifty-six men who listed a religious affiliation were Anglican. The next largest group was Catholic, all of whom served on the *Britomart*. Six of these men were Irish; the seventh was from Northumberland. There is a certain irony in the presence of Irish-Catholic sailors on a gunboat assigned to protect Canadian waters against the Fenians, and there is also a bit of a puzzle. Was it mere coincidence that all these men were aboard the *Britomart*? Might it have been a case of Alington being more tolerant of religious differences?

Marital status was given for eighty-two of the men, with thirty-four reporting that they were married and forty-eight reporting that they were single. Their average age was twenty-seven years. Aboard the *Britomart*, twenty-eight of forty-one men whose age was listed were thirty or younger; on the *Cherub*, twenty-four of thirty-six; on the *Heron*, twenty-one of thirty-eight were under thirty.[18]

Most of the crew were between 5'6" and 5'8" tall,

about average for the time. The two shortest were W.R.L. Williams of the *Heron*, who stood 4'8" at the age of sixteen, and James Curtis of the *Cherub*, who was 4'10" at the age of eighteen. The tallest member of any of the crews was William Spellman, a 5'11" black from Antigua who served aboard the *Heron*. He is clearly identifiable in photographs of the crew on the ice in Toronto harbour because of his height.

Some form of photography had been around for years, but the craft was just beginning to have dramatic impact on society. As yet, photographs were not included in personnel records, which instead consisted of brief descriptions that gave very little information for locating a missing sailor. Often, the descriptions were limited to two or three phrases: "Fair complexion, hazel eyes, light brown hair" in the case of James Gallow, the engine servant aboard the *Cherub* or "dark complexion, hazel eyes, dark brown hair" in the case of John Paul, a marine aboard the *Heron*. Scars and other distinguishing marks made identification far easier. These included tattoos, which had been associated with sailors since the 1780s when members of Captain James Cook's crew had themselves tattooed in remembrance of their visit to Polynesia. Over time, the tattoos took on specific meanings. A turtle tattoo, for example, meant a sailor had crossed the equator, while a dragon indicated a tour of duty near China. Others had religious significance or were good luck talismans meant to keep the sailors safe.[19]

A number of the men aboard the British gunboats had apparently known no other life but the sea. The records of thirteen men aboard the *Heron* were listed as having been "brought up to sea." Six of them were from Devonshire or Cornwall. Both William Spellman and John Digby Palmer, the only other black man among the crews, fell into this category. Palmer gave his place of origin as Kingston, Jamaica, but was living in Devonport when he signed on the *Heron*. On the *Britomart*, twenty-one sailors gave the sea as their occupation; five of these were from Devon or Cornwall. In contrast, only three men on the *Cherub* gave their occupations: James Bull, the warrant officer's servant, had been a bookbinder; Thomas Smith, the carpenter's mate, trained as a carpenter; and Robert Unsworth, who was an acting corporal with the RMLI, had been a collier. Not one man on the *Cherub* is listed as having previous seafaring experience, and while this may be simply a matter of gaps in the record, it may also explain some of the discipline problems that plagued the boat.

Aside from a few details on physical appearance and height, very little information was provided on the state of crew members' health. One exception had to do with smallpox: Personnel records list twenty-four men who had been vaccinated, two of whom had also had smallpox. Another three had also survived the disease, but there was no mention of whether they had been vaccinated. As long as the men appeared fit, it seems, they were signed on. However, some of them did develop health problems while serving on the gunboats. William Page, twenty-eight, was sent home from the *Heron* because of rheumatism in September 1866. A month later, twenty-five-year-old James Anderson, also of the *Heron*, was invalided home, with no reason given. Richard Goodall, twenty-three, was sick before the *Britomart* reached the Great Lakes. Although the boat's log notes that he returned from sick quarters on July 5, 1866, he was invalided out and sent to HMS *Aurora* on September 27. On August 12, 1867, thirty-five-year-old Isaac George Coleman of the *Cherub* was invalided home. A year later, another

Cherub sailor, twenty-seven-year-old Robert Dymond, was invalided for "debility" on September 18 and discharged on September 21 to the *Constance*.

At least four men died during the gunboats' Canadian sojourn. Patrick Doyle, a private in the RMLI attached to the *Cherub*, died June 8, 1868, while the boat was on Lake Ontario and was buried in Toronto. Thomas Smith, a carpenter's mate aboard the *Cherub*, died in a Toronto hospital on January 22, 1868, a month before his forty-fifth birthday. John Paul, a marine attached to the *Heron*, accidentally drowned under unusual circumstances (which we'll discuss in the next chapter), and George Dean, a thirty-two-year-old marine corporal on the *Britomart*, died in Dunnville on April 20, 1868.[20]

No details have been found about the cause of Dean's death, but his passing was reported in Dunnville's *Luminary*. The newspaper began by briefly summarizing his career. Originally trained as a turner, Dean was fair-skinned with grey eyes and brown hair. He had joined the marines in Yeofil, Somerset, on November 21, 1855, was made corporal in July 1863 and "bore an excellent character." The funeral was attended by the *Britomart* crew, a detachment of volunteer militia and "a large and respectable number of the citizens of this Village."[21] The funeral services were conducted by Reverend John Flood, the same Anglican minister who had attended the reception for the *Britomart* crew in November 1866. Following the service, Dean was buried with full military honours beside the Grand River in Dunnville's Riverside Cemetery.

Aside from his shipmates, it is likely that few of the people who attended Dean's funeral had made his acquaintance. Many, however, turned out in tribute to the George Dean who was a symbol of British military and naval might, believing it was their patriotic duty to honour a man who had died in the service of the empire. Similar demonstrations probably took place in Toronto when the other sailors died, although no record has been discovered.[22]

***

Funerals were a rare break in the humdrum routine that prevailed on the gunboats.[23] Even though the sailors' mandate was to defend Canadians against Fenian invaders, alarms were few and far between and punctuated by long periods of calm. Keeping the men occupied was important for maintaining discipline. First of all, the boat had to be kept in good repair, with broken or wormy wood replaced regularly and paint or whitewash applied. All the vessel's equipment had to be looked after as well, including ropes, guns and other machinery. And cleanliness was paramount. Hygiene was extremely important aboard ship because of the confined quarters, which allowed the rapid spread of disease. Scrubbing the deck every day helped to some extent, although some of the water inevitably seeped below decks, where, combined with the heat and moisture given off by three dozen or more men, conditions became extremely humid. By the 1850s, navy medical men were recommending that sand or sawdust be used to scrub the decks, a practice that was slowly gaining popularity.[24]

Personal hygiene was also a consideration. Victorian sailors may not have bathed as frequently as the average 21st-century Canadian, but they did wash their clothing regularly. One of the reasons for this was to control lice, which had been blamed for the cholera epidemics that ravaged the army and navy during the Crimean War.[25]

An analysis of the *Britomart* log shows that during her first year in Canadian waters, the hammocks were scrubbed about every three weeks. Clothing was washed as often as every third or fourth day, except during certain periods in the winter when the weather likely made this difficult. New clothes were sewn and existing clothes repaired at least every second week, sometimes more often, and the hammocks were repaired regularly as well.

Aside from housekeeping and maintenance tasks, the gunboat crews had to practise various drills. For example, on the morning of September 26, 1866, when the boat was in Dunnville, the men were drilled in the use of pistols; in the afternoon, they switched to small arms. The following day, Alington ordered the boat out into Lake Erie where the crew "[e]xercised Great Guns, firing shot & shells at target,"[26] the log reports. The target was made of two yards of blue bunting.

Judging by the log, it appears some effort was to made to hold regular firearms drills when the gunboats first reached the Great Lakes, but the need to put in an appearance at various ports got in the way. Still, drills took place about half-a-dozen times a month, except in December, when either inclement weather or the need of adjusting to winter quarters cut back drills to just three occasions. This changed dramatically after New Year's, likely because the men had so much more time on their hands. In January 1867, the *Britomart* log lists drills on at least nine occasions between the second of the month and the thirty-first, and February was even busier, with twelve instances.

Winters were a difficult time for the men. Making sure the men were occupied was far easier when navigation was open, and this may have been one of the reasons why naval crews typically were withdrawn from northern waters during the winter months. The *Prince Alfred* (formerly the *Michigan*) and *Rescue*, for example, were anchored for the winter and their crews sent east by train to larger ships. This left the two Canadian gunboats in the care of the *Cherub* and *Britomart*, respectively, as Lord Monck was adamant that the British gunboats remain in Canada: the *Britomart* in Dunnville, the *Cherub* in Goderich and the *Heron* in Toronto.[27] Security was the reason behind this decision: If the Fenians decided to invade again, it would make good strategic sense to strike as soon as the lakes were free of ice. The *Britomart* could protect the Grand River and the Welland Canal, which was connected to the Grand by the feeder canal that flowed through Dunnville; the *Rescue* could provide backup as soon as a crew could be put aboard. Similarly, the *Cherub* and *Prince Alfred* could protect the area around Goderich and the St. Clair River. To accommodate this, the British vessels were winterized by closing in each ship's deck with lumber, thus expanding the quarters somewhat and offering some protection from the elements. In 1866, appropriate plans were drawn up by William Irving, a Toronto architect; they called for "a cover over the deck, at a distance of about four feet from the bulworks [*sic*], with a side partition to fill up the intervening space."[28]

The British gunboats were housed-in by the end of November each year; by the end of February, the crew was at work preparing them for a new season on the lakes; by the end of March, the wooden housing had been removed from the decks.[29]

This arrangement meant that, for at least four months of the year, the sailors on the three gunboats lived in unusually close quarters in small provincial ports, with relatively little to occupy their time. Although there were occasional alarms, alerts that Fenian invasions were imminent, the sailors aboard the gunboats had few opportunities to behave as heroes. When they did, however, their actions drew attention and were widely reported in the newspapers.

One of the first incidents took place in December 1866, during a gale in Toronto harbour. On the afternoon of Saturday, December 8, the schooner *Rapid* was on her way from Hamilton to Kingston with a heavy load of iron for the Great Western Railway. Unable to outrun the storm, she put in to Toronto harbour, but stuck fast on a sandbar opposite Queen's wharf, near Toronto Island. For a time, it looked like she would sink, but Lieutenant Stephenson of the *Heron* organized a volunteer crew and got her free. Although her rudder was broken in the process, causing her to hit the wharf, damage the lighthouse, and then drift a bit, the harm was actually minimal, and the *Rapid* was able to continue her voyage and make her delivery.[30]

The following April, the *Britomart* had just reached Port Dover after the ice went out on Lake Erie. As they sailed into the harbour, a house owned by a Mr. Skey caught fire. The crew promptly rushed to the assistance of the volunteer firefighters. A few weeks later, the *Britomart* was about two miles west of Port Stanley harbour when a sailboat containing a man named Berry and three boys capsized in a sudden squall. As soon as Lieutenant Alington saw what had happened, he had a boat lowered and sent to the small group clinging to the capsized vessel. In very short order, the drenched passengers were brought to safety. There is no mention of the incident the *Britomart* log, which does list carbine drill and "employed as requisite" among the day's activities. A newspaper, however, published details on the rescue: "Too much praise cannot be given to Lieut. Allington [sic] and his gallant crew for their prompt and timely help," wrote the *London Free Press*.[31]

Newspapers were even more effusive in their praise of a member of the *Heron* crew in September 1868. Edmund VanKoughnet, a son of Phillip VanKoughnet, chancellor of the Court of Chancery of Upper Canada, was a midshipman aboard the *Heron* when she was in Brockville in September 1868. The gunboat was anchored at the wharf when a ten-year-old boy fell into the water. Although a number of other people were in the vicinity, it was his twelve-year-old brother who jumped in to try to save him a few moments later, but both were pulled under by the current. VanKoughnet, who was among those on the wharf, dove in and kept both boys afloat until a boat could pick them up. Although newspaper reports praised the older boy's courage, it was VanKoughnet who was hailed as the true hero for his "manly and courageous" act, which "deserves to be recorded."[32] The rescue was not mentioned in the ship's log, but VanKoughnet, who transferred to the *Constance* before the year was out, went on to a long and illustrious naval career which, among other things, included serving with Canadian boatmen in the Nile expedition in 1884–85 in an effort to relieve the siege of Khartoum.

Of course, not every sailor was a hero, and a number of them could fairly be described as troublemakers. It is possible that, out of a sense of patriotism, newspapers suppressed a number of stories that reflected negatively on the gunboat crews. Nevertheless, some criticism did show up from time to time. When the crews of the *Rescue* and *Prince Alfred* passed through Toronto on their way to eastern Canada

in November 1866, the *Daily Leader* complained that the
sailors, who had been provided with hot tea from the *Heron*
while waiting for the train on the platform at Union Station,
also received "perhaps a little too much whiskey from their
friends." The station was under renovation because of new
arrangements between the Grand Trunk and Great Western
railways; the presence of the sailors may have added to the
general chaos.[33] There was no comment on the quantity of
alcoholic refreshment given the officers, who were sent a
champagne supper by the officers of the 13th Hussars. But,
then, it was not the officers who tended to create most of
the discipline problems. And, even if problems did not come
to the attention of the public, they definitely had to be dealt
with on a regular basis, although one gets the impression that
the newspapers much preferred to report on the more playful
side of seafaring life. It's easy to imagine Kingston residents
having a little chuckle as they read an October 1866 report
on the *Heron*'s "jolly dogs":

> The crew of the gunboat Heron have been let out
> on leave in squads at night during the present week,
> and a jolly time they have had. Not committing
> anything like depredations, but getting into all
> kinds of such mischief as kittens might take to
> naturally. At an early hour this morning several of
> them arrayed themselves in the hides and sheepskins
> set out in front of the market square, taking good
> care that the horns were in their proper positions,
> and having danced several fandangoes on the
> side-walk disrobed and started off in search of
> "fresh fields and pasture new," wherein to gambol
> out the remainder of their furlough.[34]

Similarly, the citizens of Goderich probably smiled in January 1867 as they read about other antics:

> A battle in the snow-ba[l]ling line took place on the square one day this week between a number of boys and four sailors belonging to the Cherub, whose bared throats formed an excellent mark. The navy triumphed over the land forces, to the great amusement of on-lookers.[35]

Even though the newspapers clearly relished accounts of the "jolly tars'" daily life, there was absolutely no suggestion that duty took a back seat to recreation. In February 1867, Thomas Messenger of the *Grand River Sachem* visited the *Britomart* in Dunnville, where she was frozen in for the winter. The "staunch and trim little craft . . . would be an ugly customer for the Fenians to attack, even in her ice-bound state. Everything is in readiness for work, in case of necessity, and there is no laxity on the part of either officers or crew . . ."[36]

Readiness was the watchword of the day, a key component in reassuring Canadians that they were well protected. So, even when the initial excitement of the gunboats' arrival had died down, newspapers kept an eye on the vessels and their crews' activities and passed the word along to readers, who undoubtedly were reassured to read that the sailors of the Royal Navy continued to stand on guard. Typical of this was a brief report that appeared in the *Hamilton Evening Times* towards the end of March 1867, noting that 118 marines and ten officers had reached Toronto by special train from Quebec. The sailors had been attached to HMS *Aurora* and were on their way to man the gunboats that had been left empty and in the charge of *Britomart, Cherub* and *Heron* over the winter months.[37]

Heron *Gunboat, seen here full-masted but sails down.*

A Heron *firing party in Spring of 1867. No matter the location or the climate, firing practice was obligatory and frequent.*

Lieutenant Commander L.B. Sully of the Heron. *After his time in the Great Lakes, Solly continued to serve in the British Navy in the Caribbean and Europe.*

Lieutenant Commander Arthur Alington of the Britomart. *After his Canadian service, Alington enjoyed a long career, serving in both Africa and the Mediterranean before retiring to his family home.*

Officers and crew of Britomart *stationed on Lake Erie. The "Jolly Tars" were warmly received in the local communities and often dressed in their best and went ashore to enjoy the hospitality.*

The Heron in the Toronto Harbour, closed in for the winter and frozen in the harbour from November 1867 to April 1868.

Crew inside the closed in Heron. *Harsh winters obliged the crew to build wood paneling around the boats to protect them from the elements. What was an open ship became an enclosed fortress, where the men were obliged to stay indoors for the long winter months.*

CHAPTER 7
Discipline and Desertion

Maintaining discipline aboard ship was vital but not always easy. Routine chores definitely helped keep crews in line, although the sheer boredom of some of the tasks could sometimes be overwhelming. The *Britomart*, *Cherub* and *Heron* were stationed at small provincial ports during their sojourns in Canada, which meant daily life was pretty humdrum. And it became particularly difficult in the winter, when the crews were housed in very close quarters for at least three to four months of the year. A bit of action involving the enemy — even if it was a false alarm — could work wonders, but as naval and military men throughout history have long known, all too often daily routines were a matter of "hurry up and wait." Ultimately, it did not matter. What was paramount was that the ship ran well, that the men obeyed orders — as told, when told — and that there was a public perception of good order. While many measures were in place to assure this, the struggle never ended. There were always temptations and diversions likely to lure sailors into shirking their duty or abandoning ship altogether. At the same time, the modern British navy was trying to make accommodations with the new professionalism and humanitarianism that had come into play.

Although the general public may not have been completely aware of all the discipline issues facing the crews, they certainly knew of some and must have had a certain amount of curiosity about just what conditions were really like aboard ship for the average sailor. A decade or so earlier, punishments had been extremely harsh, but public outcry and the consequent reforms had eliminated the worst abuses by the 1860s. By the time *Britomart*, *Cherub* and *Heron* reached Canada, commanding officers were required to carefully follow regulations when disciplining their men.

Punishment in the Royal Navy was divided into two main categories: summary punishment and court martial. Usually, the latter was reserved for more serious crimes. It was more efficient to hand out summary punishments, especially when ships were at sea or remote ports, as commanders were not required to consult their superiors for confirmation of the sentence.[1]

However, they were not free to impose any punishment they deemed fit, but were required to follow a "Table of Summary Punishments," compiled in 1862 by Captain A.P. Rider, as well as the recommendations of the Articles of War. The table listed twenty-nine punishments, beginning with the most serious — discharge with disgrace — and also explained who was exempt from certain punishments. First-class seamen, for instance, could not be flogged.[2]

Officers had to write out warrants, which included the details of the offence, the past behaviour of the offender and what punishment was decided upon. In addition, the warrant had to be signed twelve hours before the punishment was carried out.[3] This required cooling-off period allowed for sober second thought on the part of a commanding officer who might have overreacted, as well as providing some time for an inebriated or otherwise out-of-control offender to repent or apologize. As a further safeguard against brutality, the details of all punishments had to be listed in a "defaulter's book" and submitted to headquarters every three months.

The crews were regularly reminded of the standards of conduct expected and the punishments imposed for infractions through regular reading of the Articles of War. Dating back to 1661, the Articles were originally designed to prevent cowardice and disobedience on the part of officers, a crucial requirement because, as the preamble noted, "the wealth, Safety and Strength of this kingdom" depended on the navy.[4] While the wording was somewhat revised over the next two centuries, the sentiment expressed in the 1866 version was nearly identical to the 1661 version. However, the overall thrust of the Articles had evolved to meet changing conditions and shifting issues. Treason and cowardice were no longer paramount concerns. While discipline was still important, its dispensation was coloured considerably by a rising concern with the rights of the individual.

The 1866 version contained 101 clauses, starting with the requirement for public worship and observation of the Lord's Day in accordance with the liturgy of the Church of England. The subsequent forty-five clauses dealt with "Misconduct in the Presence of the Enemy," "Communication with the Enemy," "Neglect of Duty," "Insubordination,"

"Miscellaneous Offences" and "Offences Punishable by Ordinary Law." These were followed by clauses detailing what punishment was to be given and how. Although Captain Rider had listed twenty-nine summary punishments in 1862, the 1866 Articles enumerated only eleven, including those imposed following court martial. From most to least serious, they were death; penal servitude; dismissal with disgrace; imprisonment or corporal punishment; dismissal; forfeiture of seniority as an officer; dismissal from the ship; severe reprimand or reprimand; disrating (demotion); forfeiture of some or all pay, other remuneration or medals and decorations; and a final catch-all category for "minor Punishments" dictated by naval custom.

Death could only be imposed if at least two-thirds of the officers involved in a court martial agreed with the verdict, unless only five officers presided, in which case four of them had to agree. Execution could then follow in the case of mutiny, but for any other offence the sentence had to be confirmed by the admiralty or, at the very least, by the commander-in-chief of a foreign station.[5] Penal servitude could be imposed for anywhere from five years to life and automatically involved discharge with disgrace, while imprisonment could only be imposed for two years. However, a sentence of imprisonment could also call for additional punishment, such as solitary confinement or hard labour. Aside from depriving sailors of their liberty, some of the punishments also hit them in the pocketbook. Dismissal with disgrace resulted in automatic forfeiture of all pay and other moneys due, such as bounties, salvage and prize money, as well as relinquishment of medals and other honours. Depriving a sailor of a good conduct badge usually resulted in a reduction in pay. Furthermore, if a sailor deserted, anything he left behind on the ship was no longer considered his property.

The Articles of War were supposed to be posted in prominent locations on the ships. Some commanders, including Lieutenant Alington, recognized that the literacy level of their crew members varied widely and regularly read aloud sections of the Articles. In addition, Alington read periodic reports about punishments that had recently been meted out on various ships throughout the navy.[6] There was little chance that a sailor could successfully plead ignorance of his infractions as an excuse.

Available records indicate that twenty-seven men on the three gunboats were disciplined in some manner between August 1866 and November 1868: three on the *Britomart*, five on the *Heron* and nineteen on the *Cherub*. Nine were deprived of good conduct badges; four were reduced in rank. One of the latter, John Roberts of the *Cherub*, had already been deprived of a good conduct badge on April 30, 1867, prior to being reduced on September 3, 1867. Benjamin Stanley, also of the *Cherub*, lost a good conduct badge and was sentenced to fourteen days in jail on May 7, 1868, for an unspecified offence. Henry Spriggs, another *Cherub* sailor, not only lost a good conduct badge and was reduced in rank, but was also sentenced to forty-two days in prison at hard labour. This occurred on January 28, 1868. About two months after his release, he was in trouble again and this time was sentenced to fourteen days in jail.

Many of the offences reported involved drunkenness. At the time, civilians might routinely be sentenced to a night or a week in jail for similar offences,[7] but naval regulations apparently called for harsher punishments.[8] William Lee of the *Cherub* spent three terms in Goderich jail for drunkenness;[9] George Sheppard spent forty-two days in the same jail for the same offence,[10] as did his shipmates Samuel Taylor[11] and Thomas Webb.[12]

The dates of their sentencing suggest all three might have been celebrating the new year together. Usually, convictions for drunkenness were handled routinely, but sometimes they escalated into more serious offences. Such was the case with *Cherub* gunner Edward Rowse, who was arrested and severely reprimanded for drunkenness on September 9, 1866. The tersely worded entries in the gunboat log note that Rowse was arrested at 11:40 on a Sunday morning, apparently confined on the ship (possibly to sleep off his spree), then "severely reprimanded" for drunkenness and disrespect by Lieutenant Huntley in the presence of several officers at 1 p.m. on Monday. He was then released. Following a similar offence on September 28, a Friday, he was arrested at 6:40 p.m., then placed under close arrest at 8:55 p.m., released from close arrest Saturday morning at 11:50 and then set free Sunday at 10:25 a.m.[13] Presumably Rowse got out of control when drinking, perhaps becoming violent. The following month, Captain De Horsey boarded the *Cherub* to hold a court of inquiry into Rowse's behaviour. The results were not reported in the log or the local newspapers.[14]

The strong influence alcohol had on desertion and discipline problems is emphasized by the behaviour of naval prisoners during their periods of incarceration. Although its records are patchy, the Huron County Jail in Goderich augments the *Cherub* log and newspaper reports to some extent. Between October 6, 1866, and August 1868, seven men were listed in both the jail records and elsewhere. With the exception of George Shepphard, who was twenty-two in August 1867, all the men were well behaved while in jail, presumably because they were sober. Sheppard, however, is listed as a discipline problem and "intemperate," suggesting he was able to easily obtain more liquor than was good for him.

Victorian reformers saw a correlation between lack of education and law-breaking, and so periodically tracked literacy levels of prisoners. All of the *Cherub* prisoners claimed they could read and write, although how well is debatable. Jail officials almost certainly relied on the men's own assessment of their literacy levels, and only George Shepphard's record makes it clear that he could read and write "imperfectly." The understanding of a connection between illiteracy and lawbreaking may have been what underlay series of entries in the *Britomart* log. For several days during the winter of 1866–67, it was reported that a party went to school. There is a remote possibility that the men were working on some kind of construction project, but at the time it was not unusual for boys in their late teens and young men to attend classes during the winter months, when they could be spared from farm work. Alington almost certainly would have sanctioned such a plan for his men's self-improvement.

Religious affiliation and martial status were also recorded, but again officials had to rely on the prisoners' accuracy, which apparently varied widely, as demonstrated in the case of William Lee. Lee, who claimed to be thirty-six, single, literate, and a member of the Church of England when first incarcerated in Goderich in early October 1866, had acquired a wife and child by the second term in jail in February 1867 and lost them by the time he was arrested again on May 2. He had also switched religious affiliation to the Church of Scotland, which he maintained at the time of his third arrest.

While it is possible Lee had suffered a domestic tragedy in the early months of 1867, the sudden appearance and disappearance of a family more strongly suggests a common-law arrangement of some type, one that could be ended quickly by either party.[15]

Occasionally, commanders resorted to flogging offenders. This was one of the punishments that had been criticized by those calling for naval reforms, but was still implemented from time to time. Some sailors considered it preferable to a jail term, as it was over and done with more quickly, and according to Michael Lewis, most marines were flogged at one point or another. Inevitably, it became somewhat routine, accepted as simply a part of a marine's lot, and it was apparently not unusual for a man to suffer calmly through four dozen lashes with an air of detachment, as though the whole process were happening to someone else. Like any other unpleasant activity, it was best dealt with as calmly and expeditiously as possible before moving on to other things.[16]

This did not mean that there weren't those who considered flogging barbaric and their number was growing. Noting that one of his shipmates received four dozen lashes on the morning of November 16, 1865, John Tilling commented, "I wonder if the society for prevention of cruelty to animals could not interfere and put a stop to these disgraceful floggings."[17] Flogging was finally suspended for peacetime offences in 1871, but remained in force during wartime until 1879.[18]

Generally, flogging was reserved for the most serious offences and could not be administered to officers. The gunboat logs do not specify what the offences were, but at least four sailors were flogged during the three gunboats' tour of duty in Canada. On August 16, 1866, William Lee received the maximum, forty-eight lashes. Lee was sent to jail five times between October 1866 and May 1867, suggesting he was a serious discipline problem. Arthur Septimus Lloyd, a sailor on the *Britomart*, was flogged soon after the gunboat put into Port Dalhousie for repairs.[19] It was the second time on the initial voyage to the Great Lakes that Lloyd was flogged, the first having occurred at 11:30 on the morning of August 10, the day after the *Britomart* was damaged going through the Lachine Canal. It is impossible to determine whether the two events are related, but perhaps Lieutenant Alington was highly frustrated because of the mishap and less tolerant of Lloyd's behaviour. The twenty- one-year-old Lloyd was from Marleybone, London, and claimed to have been brought up to the sea, but seemed to be a discipline problem. Another who was flogged was Samuel Taylor, who had previously been jailed for drunkenness. He received thirty-six lashes on December 12, 1867. Finally, Frederick Stanford received thirty-six lashes and was "discharged to shore with disgrace."[20] The only other offences listed are "selling clothes belonging to HM" (which brought William Lee a twenty-eight-day jail sentence),[21] "leaving ship" or "breaking out of ship" without permission and desertion.

In spite of the image of the "jolly tars" who dutifully served the British cause, unauthorized absences and desertions were a very serious problem, as we will discuss shortly. But first some other aspects of discipline should be considered.

Newspaper readers were probably amused at antics such as snowball fights and dressing up in animal hides, but some of the sailors' activities had a more sinister side. In June 1868, a fight broke out between a sailor from the *Cherub* and some "roughs" in Prescott,[22] and one of them fractured the sailor's skull with a stone. At first there were fears that he would succumb to his injury. This report may have raised a little more concern than a typical brawl because it pitted Royal Navy sailors against unidentified hoodlums. In general, there seems to have been more general tolerance of fighting and petty crimes if both the perpetrators and the victims belonged to the same social milieu. But an attack on a British sailor was also, at some level, an attack on the empire he represented. Fortunately, by the time the incident was reported in the papers, the sailor was recovering.[23]

As stated previously, one of the challenges facing the commanders of the *Britomart*, *Heron* and *Cherub* was keeping their crews occupied. Social events and parades and the rare rumour of a Fenian incursion provided some excitement, but generally the sailors' lives were a monotonous routine of maintaining the ship, cleaning and repairing their clothes, drills and target practice. They could not even count on regular shore leave, as this was left to the commander's discretion.[24] During the first weeks on the Great Lakes, there was no leave for gunboat crews because of continuing concern about a possible Fenian attack. By September, however, Lieutenant Alington was relaxed enough to grant special and privileged leave four times, on September 16, 20, 28, and 30.[25] Two of those days were Sundays; it became routine for Alington to grant leave on Sundays whenever possible. The *Heron* crew had leave in Kingston on September 4 and 5, with one watch alternating each day, but nothing is noted for the *Cherub*. Over the next two months, the only leave noted in the logs are for the *Britomart*, with all three coming in late October. After that, however, the *Britomart* crew was granted leave at least twice a month, and sometimes more frequently. In July 1867, for instance, special and privileged leave was arranged six times.

By comparison, instances of leave for the *Cherub* and *Heron* were few and far between; twice a month or less for both of them until June 1867. At that point, the *Cherub* commander adopted a strategy similar to Alington's and offered regular special and privileged leave, usually on a Sunday. (It must be stressed that the sailors of the *Heron* probably went on leave more frequently than the log book indicates. For instance, the sailor who got into the altercation in Prescott, discussed above, was almost certainly on leave, but there is no corresponding mention of leave in the log.)

Shore leave provided a welcome break from routine for the sailors and probably lifted morale. But it also gave the men opportunities to get into trouble that resulted in disciplinary action. Two days after a general leave was granted to the starboard watch of the *Cherub* in January 1867, Thomas Webb, Samuel Taylor, William Lee and Patrick Doyle were all sentenced to jail terms.[26] The day after general leave was given to the *Cherub*'s port watch on April 3, 1867, Private J. Hubbard, RMLI, was sentenced to forty-two days in prison.[27] On October 17, 1867, special and privileged leave was granted to the *Britomart* crew in Dunnville; the following day, boatswain's mate Henry Chambers was deprived of one good conduct badge.[28] A few months later, after another Sunday leave was granted the crew, stoker Michael Young was sent to jail for twenty-one days.[29]

Discipline problems on the *Britomart* were apparently few and far between. The log is very detailed, suggesting any problems that did occur were recorded. In addition, retired sea captain Alexander McNeilledge noted in his diary that there was "good discipline" on board the *Britomart* and that Alington had the respect of his men.[30] Because of the comparative lack of detail in the *Heron* log, it is difficult to determine the level of discipline on board that gunboat. The *Cherub*, however, seems to have had a particularly fractious crew. Although the reasons are not quite clear, some possibilities emerge through close examination of the personnel records. Three of the *Cherub* men who received jail sentences were marines, Patrick Doyle, William Lee and George Sheppard; the last two were repeat offenders with three and four jail terms each, although Lee was well behaved once he was incarcerated and sober.

As Michael Lewis states, marines, who were called "lobsters" because of their red coats, were stereotyped as heavy drinkers and more likely to need discipline. They tended to come from the lowest of labouring families or from the countryside and were not necessarily the most competent of seafaring men. While they were usually quite willing to follow orders, they were not noted for thinking for themselves or considering the consequences of such actions as drinking too much, falling asleep on sentry duty or fighting with their shipmates. They rarely became embroiled in major offences such as mutiny, but got into trouble often enough to be stereotyped for it.

Aside from the marines, sixteen other men on the *Cherub* were also disciplined, some severely. It is possible that there was a morale problem onboard, or the commander was incompetent or inexperienced. It is interesting to note that of the twenty-nine offences recorded, only ten were recorded after June 1867, when more frequent shore leave was introduced. This tactic, which had been tried as early as the 1840s, had been proven to reduce desertion and improve discipline, and it definitely seems to have worked aboard the *Cherub*.[31]

But there is another possible explanation for the discipline problems aboard this particular gunboat. The origins of the *Cherub* crew were significantly different from those on board the other two gunboats. Of the men who served on the *Britomart* whose origins can be traced, sixteen were from Cornwall and Devon, and all six of the Irishmen aboard were from Cork. In Cornwall and Devon, some families had gone to sea for generations, either in the merchant marine or in the regular navy. Often, sailors from the same geographic area who shipped out together were related, or at the very least, known to each other, and aboard ship they might form a tight-knit community that transmitted its skill and culture to less experienced members of the crew. There might be rivalries between different factions on the ship — for example, between Devonshire men and those from Cork — but because there was a definite sense of cohesion among crew members, certain standards of behaviour were imposed from within, and the collective good tended to take precedence over that of the individual. With the men on the *Cherub* coming from all over England, and the largest group coming from Hampshire, rather than Cornwall or Devon, it appears that it was more difficult than usual to foster camaraderie and good order onboard.[32]

The reduction in offences after June 1867, while attributable to increased shore leave, may also have resulted from the crew members finally having developed some kind of community spirit after a year or so together. This may also indicate that the commander had picked up a certain degree of skill in the interim, reflected in better discipline among the crew.

Yet, even if a crew's morale was generally good, there were always individuals who flouted the rules, including some who deserted. Desertion was a serious offence, not only because it reduced the available manpower and affected morale, but also because deserters might possess information that could be of advantage to the enemy. "Desertion has always been rife in Canada," Algernon De Horsey wrote in 1866.[33] Merchant vessels generally paid higher wages than the navy, and many sailors gladly risked punishment in order to improve their incomes. In her study of merchant sailors in eastern Canada, Judith Fingard notes that there were so many desertions in 1861 that the admiral "threatened to search every merchant vessel leaving Halifax for his missing men."[34] That almost certainly would not have been practical, but there were measures put in place for dealing with desertions, outlined by De Horsey in April 1867, including the practice of telegraphing descriptions of the deserters to various authorities.

In May 1867, Captain Thomas Cochrane reported eleven desertions from *Prince Alfred* and two from *Hercules*.[35] Responding to the report, Vice-Admiral Sir James Hope commented that desertions were attributable "too frequently in a great measure to the want of proper care on the part of the officers."[36]

Ironically, less than a month previously, De Horsey had issued a memo regarding desertions and called for extra vigilance on the part of officers.[37] Noting that "the temptations held out for desertion are very great both at Quebec and Montreal, and also at the River and Lake Ports," he advised officers not to keep boats down after sunset in order to minimize the opportunities for jumping ship.[38]

Deserters automatically faced court martial. Although the maximum penalty for desertion during wartime was death, in most cases deserters received prison sentences. Canadian newspapers frequently published reports of desertion, partly because the topic was newsworthy, but also to remind readers of the punishments facing deserters and those who aided them. Some newspapers even went so far as to publish information on rewards that would be paid to those helping to bring deserters to justice and the punishments prescribed for those assisting them. Anyone who persuaded a sailor to desert, hid him or helped in other ways could be fined or sentenced to up to two years in prison or the penitentiary at hard labour, at the discretion of the court.[39]

At least one Ontarian learned first-hand about the consequences of helping a deserter: In the fall of 1867, John Patterson, a farmer living in Nottawasaga, near Georgian Bay, was charged at the Barrie assizes for harbouring a navy deserter. Lieutenant Solly of the *Heron* appeared for the prosecution at the trial on October 10, which resulted in a sentence of two months at hard labour for Patterson.[40]

The amount of the rewards for turning over a deserter varied, starting with three pounds, fifteen shillings for bringing deserters to the authorities, an additional sum for travelling expenses and compensation for "[t]he loss of time, expense or difficulty . . . in the apprehension of a deserter." That did not prevent the navy from being niggardly. When William Harkness, chief of police in an unnamed town, tried to claim mileage expenses in conjunction with apprehension of deserters, Hope instructed De Horsey to "acquaint" Harkness with the fact his request was "expressly prohibited" by admiralty regulations.[41] For 1867, the reward was increased to £7, but only if a deserter was apprehended within two months. After that it dropped to £2, then to a maximum of £1 after six months. No reward was paid for turning in a deserter after a year had passed.[42]

In October 1866, the *Daily Leader* reported on a deserter, McAdam Robinson, formerly of the Royal Marines, who was taken into custody near Queenston. Robinson had joined an American regiment and was serving as a corporal, but "did not feel comfortable among the Yankees" and surrendered to authorities. He was transported by train under armed guard to Toronto to stand trial.[43] John Hawkin deserted the *Cherub* on October 27, 1866, but was captured, jailed and transferred to HMS *Niger* to await trial on November 14.[44] Two sailors on the *Britomart* deserted in January 1867. According to the log, Nicholas Fleming and Henry Gilbard apparently remained at large during the *Britomart*'s time in Canada.[45] Fleming's record says "absent without leave," while Gilbard's states "broken out of ship"; since both disappearances occurred on the same day, it is possible they colluded. This was certainly the case with two sailors aboard the *Hercules*. One of them deserted and was arrested and confined on the ship while it was in Prescott. During the night, the sailor assigned to guard him decided to desert as well. Together, they lowered a boat and headed for the American side of the river. Although their absence was noticed soon afterwards, the pursuers were unable to catch them. In reporting the event, the *Prescott Telegraph* editorialized, "We [report] such desertions with sincere regret because one has always been accustomed to regard a British seaman as the very soul of manly honor and of devoted loyalty to his country's flag."[46]

In spite of the sentiments expressed by the newspaper, it was not difficult to find examples of a distinct absence of honour among British seamen, including officers. One case that received extensive coverage was that of George Greenall Boys, an acting sub-lieutenant who left the gunboat *Royal* while she was in Cornwall. His court martial, which was held in England, was reported on the front page of Toronto's *Daily Leader*.

Boys belonged to a navy family. His father was a

captain and veteran of the Crimean War. His brother was a first lieutenant and his great-uncle was Admiral George Sayer. Despite these illustrious connections, Boys failed to return from leave on September 6, 1866. His whereabouts were apparently unknown until he surrendered to Commodore Edmondstone in Woolwich, England, on February 6, 1867. According to testimony presented, Boys had been worried about debts he owed a number of people and claimed he could not pay because his bank had failed. He was also concerned the he would be arrested for debt while in Canada. "This would have been my ruin," he said in a statement to the court, "for it involved not merely incarceration in an obscure Canadian prison, where I should have been left a total stranger when my ship had sailed, but the degrading companionship of rebels and outcasts of the vilest description."

Apparently Boys was so appalled at the prospect of being imprisoned alongside Fenian invaders that he ran — from his creditors, he insisted, not from his "noble profession." Ironically, his fears might have been totally unjustified. Writing from the *Aurora* at Quebec in April 1867, De Horsey stated that "naval prisoners" would be incarcerated at military prisons in Quebec, Montreal and Toronto, providing there was room;[47] otherwise, they would go to a common jail. Even if he was jailed, Boys might have never run into any Fenians.

Ultimately, Boys hoped to throw himself on the mercy of his superior officers in England and thus avoid "the contamination and absolute pollution of a Canadian prison." He planned to make his way back to England via New York, but fell ill there. By the time he had recovered, he was out of money. After some time, he found work on a Prussian ship in exchange for passage to Antwerp. The voyage took seven weeks, during which the mate knocked him senseless with a belaying pin; the injury resulted in another delay in Antwerp before he finally headed for England and surrendered himself to authorities at Woolwich. At the trial three weeks later, Boys cited the "exceptional trial and peculiar hardships" he had experienced as he pleaded for a chance to make amends. After a brief deliberation, the court ruled that the charge of desertion had been "fully proved," but in light of Boys's ordeal waived any punishment except dismissal from the navy.[48]

Boys received lenient treatment because he had turned himself in to the authorities, expressed regret and had naval connections. Not every deserter was as fortunate. In June 1867, an unnamed sailor passed through Toronto on his way to begin a four-year prison term. According to a report in the Toronto *Globe*, he was one of thirteen men aboard the *Rescue* who had fled to the United States after the gunboat made her first voyage that spring. By the time he was convicted, eleven of his shipmates had returned to the *Rescue*, "the land of liberty having failed to come up to their preconceived notions and all on their return expressed themselves heartily glad to be taken back." One of the sailors who was convicted was apparently unwilling to return to the gunboat, but refused to stay in any country "where they charged a British shilling for a glass of grog."[49]

The *Globe* got at least some of its facts wrong. Thirteen sailors had indeed deserted that spring, but not from *Rescue*. Instead, correspondence from De Horsey and Hope indicate that eleven left *Prince Alfred* and another two left *Hercules*.[50] But there was definitely a great deal of truth in the newspaper's claim that "the want of proper amusement" during the winter months was the reason the men had decided to desert.

The anti-American sentiments expressed in the *Globe* article may have been more the product of the reporter's patriotic imagination than a reflection of reality, but it does appear that a number of sailors deserted or delayed their return to their vessels before reconsidering and facing up to any punishment they had coming. And in some cases, sailors who were presumed to be deserters had instead met with foul play or accidents. Such was the fate of John Paul, a private in the RMLI aboard the *Heron* who failed to return from leave in November 1866. Standing 5'6" tall, Paul had a dark complexion and hazel eyes and hailed from Somersetshire. At the time of his disappearance, he was twenty-eight and had been married for about a year. He had served on at least three other boats prior to the *Heron*, most recently the *Royal George*.

Assuming Paul had deserted, an officer filled out the appropriate paperwork. The following spring, two men from the *Heron* fell into the lake one night on their way back to the gunboat "after indulging in spirituous liquors very freely." As they bobbed about in the frigid water, each man in turn grabbed what he thought was his mate, but was actually the body of the missing marine. A coroner's inquest ruled the death accidental, and Paul was buried in the military cemetery near Fort York.[51]

In delivering their verdict, the coroner's jury noted that the road leading to the Toronto wharf was "in a very dangerous state" and a fence should be built to protect travellers.[52] The gunboat crews, as well as anyone else who used Canadian docks, were uncomfortably familiar with the hazards. In November 1866, the *Goderich Signal* reported on problems with the town's harbour:

Owing to the narrowness of the dock where the Cherub lies and the slides which are covered with ice in frosty weather several of the seamen in attempting to get aboard at night have tumbled into the river. One man fell in night before last and would have been drowned but for the fact of his being a good swimmer. Some extra precautions should be taken.[53]

Along with icy conditions, denizens of the docks often had to cope with extreme darkness. In September 1866, a taxi driver in Montreal, returning two officers to HMS *Pylades*, drove straight into the St. Lawrence. Although the wharf should have been lighted, for some reason all the lamps had been extinguished. With some difficulty, the two officers escaped from cab and tried to bring the driver to safety, but the current was too strong for them. The cabman drowned, along with his horse. Such mishaps were fairly common, but little was done to correct them. No one seemed to really want to take on the cost and responsibility of ensuring the ports were as well lighted and safe as possible. Furthermore, it was felt that sailors were ultimately responsible for their own safety. If they wished to risk life and limb by drinking heavily and then facing the hazards of a dark and possibly icy harbour, they would have to bear the consequences.

EPILOGUE
Maintaining a Presence

Aside from some isolated incidents, the gunboats saw little action during their time in Canada. The most stressful time was summer 1868, when rumours of another imminent invasion reached fever pitch. On June 10, Toronto's *Daily Leader* reported, "The several gunboats in the Canadian waters have been placed on a complete war footing. Each one has its full complement of men, and all are well armed and ready."[1] Ironically, a day earlier the *Hamilton Evening Times* observed, "the probabilities of a demonstration from the United States are growing weaker daily solely in consequence of the energy displayed by the Government in preparations to repel an attack."[2] As far as the *Evening Times* was concerned, the presence of gunboats provided ample protection against the Fenians. Furthermore, the newspaper speculated, all the talk of an invasion was an "electioneering dodge" to pressure presidential candidate General Ulysses S. Grant into enforcing neutrality laws, which would lose him the support of Fenians and their sympathizers in the fall election.[3]

Beginning in late May 1868, the gunboats were moved around more than they had been previously, suggesting something was afoot. The *Heron* was sent east to patrol the St. Lawrence near Prescott; the *Cherub* was sent from Lake Huron to Lake Ontario,[4] where she joined the *Britomart* and the *Rescue*.[5] Meanwhile, the *Prince Alfred* was posted to the Detroit River.[6] By July, the *Cherub* was back in the St. Clair River, where she ran aground on Herson's Island. Although the *Prince Alfred* was nearby, worries about a Fenian attack were so profound that, while attempts were made to lighten her and float her off the island, her guns were charged and manned and other precautions taken.[7] A month later, both the *Cherub* and the *Britomart* were in the Windsor area, leading the *Detroit Post* to comment that something was "in the wind."[8]

All this activity may have been justified if there were real concerns of another invasion. But it might also have been a political strategy on the part of those who wanted to keep the gunboats on active service in Canada. As early as the fall of 1866, British officials had considered removing the boats from Canadian waters, but acceded to the request of Governor-General Monck and others. In March 1867, the secretary of state for the colonies, Lord Carnarvon, called for a reduction of British naval presence on the Great Lakes.[9] In September 1867, Carnarvon's successor, the Duke of Buckingham, forwarded Monck a letter from Vice-Admiral Sir Rodney Mundy, who wanted to remove the gunboats that November. Monck responded by reiterating his arguments of the previous year: While there was no imminent threat of a Fenian invasion, he believed spring was the likeliest time for an attack, and it would be unwise to remove the gunboats. In February 1868, Buckingham wrote to the Canadian Privy Council about reducing naval patrols in the St. Lawrence and cancelling plans to man the Canadian gunboats with British sailors. Advised by the minister of militia, whose informants reported that a Fenian invasion was still a strong possibility, the Privy Council wrote to Lord Monck asking that the status quo be maintained. Monck agreed about the possibility of an invasion and said as much in his correspondence with Buckingham: "I consider the maintenance of gunboats on the lakes and river St. Lawrence, the most inexpensive and effective measure that could be adopted for preventing any further attack, or for repelling it, should the invasion be attempted."[10] Monck got his way, but, as it turned out, had only delayed the inevitable. In early October, the *Hamilton Evening Times* reported that orders had been given to remove the *Britomart*, *Cherub* and *Heron* from the lakes before the winter.[11] Three weeks later, the paper reported that some attempts were being made to keep the gunboats in place, "and it is not likely that they will be withdrawn."[12] The report was erroneous. Before the end of the month, the *Britomart*, *Heron* and *Cherub* had left the Great Lakes.[13]

It appears the British naval command may have vacillated a bit in its decision. According to the *New Dominion*, the *Britomart* was already making preparations for another winter on the Grand River and lumber had been purchased for housing in the boat. Then, late in October an unexpected telegram arrived, ordering her to Halifax as quickly as possible. The gunboat was in Port Dover when the orders came through, and her sudden departure was something of a shock to the townsfolk. The *New Dominion* described their feelings thus:

> We cannot wish them God speed on their way without feeling how thoroughly the officers and the men have endeared themselves to all of us, not only to the inhabitants of Port Dover, but to the community of the country at large. Thorough gentlemen for officers they were all, in every respect, a model crew and it will be long before we look upon their like again. The call was sudden and unexpected. But few were aware of their intended departure until heavy booming of the great gun smote on their ears. In one short hour all was ready, and as they rapidly steamed out of our harbor we could not help feeling that each individually had lost a friend, if not a protector. Hands were warmly shaken; the last farewell taken, and as they left our shores a rousing cheer rose from the hearts of all on shore. — Another gun; the yards were manned, and a responding cheer burst from those on board; the good ship sped on her way, and we had seen the last of the "Britomart."[14]

After making arrangements to sell the lumber for the benefit of the poor of Dunnville, the *Britomart* steamed off to the east coast.[15]

Naturally, a number of newspapers commented on the withdrawal of the gunboats. The *New Dominion* was critical of the decision:

> In losing our blue jackets we cannot but question the polity of the Government that removed them, and the policy of abandoning the command of the lakes.

True, the Fenian excitement is at an end: but we all know the temper of our neighbours across the lines. We know and feel their utter abnegation as a people of all national law when it suits them, and the greedy eye they always have on Canada. We feel it is only the quiet of a volcano ready to burst forth the first convenient opportunity. Again we say we question the wisdom of that policy which, by abandoning the command of the lakes, leaves us open to any eruption such as we have heretofore experienced, and may again.[16]

In contrast, the *Canadian News* took a more balanced view:

There has been a good deal of grumbling in the press of the dominion about the proposal to reduce the number of troops serving among us and the withdrawal of the gunboats from the lakes. We trust that the action of the Imperial authorities will neither be too sudden nor pushed too far; but, assuredly, we have had no reason to expect that our garrisons would be kept up upon the present footing much longer.[17]

CONCLUSION

When the Fenians invaded in 1866, Canadians were ill equipped to provide naval defence. Although there had been ample warning of a possible attack, the main focus had been on land forces. Even when it was determined that armed naval vessels were essential to Canadian security, it took considerable effort to persuade British authorities to assign the appropriate gunboats to the St. Lawrence River and the Great Lakes. Delays were caused by a combination of bureaucratic procrastination, concerns about violating the Rush-Bagot Agreement and adversely affecting diplomatic relations with the United States, plus financial considerations. Finally, following the invasion of June 1, 1866, Canadian and British authorities rushed to put together a navy using hired vessels hastily converted to gunboats and manned by a combination of local crews — including volunteer naval brigades — and British sailors. The result was more delays. Some boat owners bargained for the best price possible, and a certain amount of profiteering took place, notably in the case of MP and boat owner Lachlan McCallum. In addition, there were administrative foul-ups, such as the Toronto Naval Brigade sailing off aboard one of the Canadian gunboats even as British sailors were on their way to man it. Eventually, though, the temporary navy took shape, consisting of three British Britomart-class gunboats, augmented by vessels leased or purchased by the Canadian government. These were manned by sailors from the Royal Navy and backed up by other navy vessels,   such as the *Pylades*, when required.

While it is impossible to say with any certainty what might have occurred had the gunboats been in place by May 1866, subsequent events suggest that the June invasion might have been averted. Arguably, the Fenians' organizational difficulties, the arrests made following the Battle of Ridgeway and American ambiguity about the situation had a significant bearing on later Fenian activities. However, the presence of armed gunboats on Canadian waters sent a clear signal to both the Fenians and the American government that, the Rush-Bagot Agreement notwithstanding, British-Canadians were willing and capable of defending their territory. As Britain was the most powerful military and naval force in the world and the United States was dealing with serious internal issues following the Civil War, the Canadian exercise in gunboat diplomacy apparently succeeded in preventing further Fenian invasions. Precisely how effective the gunboats were in persuading the American government to enforce neutrality laws is a subject for further study.

Similarly, it would be interesting to explore why it appears the gunboats were commanded by young, relatively inexperienced officers. Did the British admiralty not take the crisis seriously? Was the choice deliberately made in order to provide a handy excuse in the event some action on the part of those officers sparked a diplomatic crisis? Or was it simply a matter of economics? Alternatively, it is possible that the admiralty assessed the situation and determined the threat was something easily handled by junior officers, who would thereby receive training that might serve them well in other trouble spots at some future date. Without further biographical information about the gunboat commanders and details as to why they were chosen to serve in Canada, those questions will go unanswered. However, what the research for this book uncovered is that gunboat diplomacy had a positive effect on Canadian morale.

If the newspapers of the 1860s accurately reflected Canadian perceptions, one of the serious effects of the Fenian invasion was the creation of a siege mentality, a certain degree of paranoia and substantial fear of the Irish. This was relieved by the arrival of the *Britomart, Cherub* and *Heron* which, despite their inability to reach the speeds of American revenue cutters, were seen as a symbol of Britain's naval power and willingness to protect Canadians. Similarly, the officers and crewmen were seen in symbolic terms, as heroic representatives of the mother country who were willing to sacrifice their lives in far-flung corners of the empire to preserve *Pax Britannic*a. However, the adulations that greeted the officers and crews in various ports, as well as the receptions and other public ceremonies, was more than an outpouring of patriotic fervor; these were also opportunities for Canadians to experience a special sense of community. Whether they toured the gunboats, attended receptions for the crews or read about these events in newspapers, it was possible for them to identify with others in distant towns, to recognize themselves as like-minded individuals and to draw comfort from the common experience that simultaneously set them apart from Fenians and Americans and bound them more strongly to Britain. Meanwhile, the officers and sailors played their parts to the hilt, as genteel, courageous warrior-diplomats and sturdy, dependable defenders of the empire.

Of course, there was a gap between perception and

reality, although it may not have been apparent to the general public at the time. De Horsey's rather heavy-handed dealings with Governor-General Lord Monck regarding chain of command indicate that diplomacy did not always come naturally to naval officers on the gunboats. In addition, the number of infractions committed by sailors, as well as numerous desertions, indicates that the "jolly jack tars" of the British navy were not always content with their working conditions. Nor were they necessarily loyal to Britain, as evidenced by those who were apparently willing to relocate to the United States after jumping ship.

During the twenty-six months the *Britomart*, *Cherub* and *Heron* were stationed on the Great Lakes, none of them engaged the enemy. There were occasional false alarms when an unidentified ship unexpectedly appeared in Canadian waters. There was a flurry of activity resulting from rumours that circulated in the months leading up to the American presidential election of 1868. But there was no serious threat to Canadian security. Various observers, from retired sea captain Alexander McNeilledge in Port Dover to British government officials in London, concluded well before the end of 1866 that the Fenians were no longer a significant danger. Yet the three small gunboats remained on the Great Lakes year-round, and, in an unprecedented decision, larger manned vessels were also ordered to winter in eastern Canada. It was an expensive undertaking, both for Britain and for the Canadian government, but one that Canadians deemed essential. That Governor-General Monck was twice able to persuade the British government to allow the *Britomart*, *Cherub* and *Heron* to remain on the Great Lakes for an additional season suggests Britain recognized the benefits of allaying Canadians' fears by providing more protection than was absolutely essential. Gunboat diplomacy aside, the reasons for this are not completely clear, at least not based on the information gathered for this book.

With the exception of descriptions of the gunboats' involvement in celebrations on July 1, 1867, there are few references to Confederation in the research. However, it is possible that the gunboats were permitted to remain on the Great Lakes as long as they did both to remind the Fenians and American authorities of Britain's might and to reinforce Canadian ties with Britain during the months immediately before and after Confederation. To hypothesize for a moment, what if *Britomart*, *Cherub* and *Heron* had been withdrawn in October 1866 and another Fenian raid ensued? Successful or not, if it had resulted in any property damage or loss of life, Britain's failure to provide the defence Canadians had requested would have been severely criticized. That in turn might have ultimately opened the door to closer political ties with the United States. Alternatively, it might have paved the way for a hostile American takeover of the new Dominion. While these scenarios are speculative, they may have been considered by the British naval administration and influenced the decision to leave the gunboats on the Great Lakes for an extended period.

To return to Michael Lewis's fanciful analogy of naval vessels and police officers, the *Britomart*, *Cherub* and *Heron* did little in the way of chasing or arresting lawbreakers. But they did provide a comforting presence and a sense of security to Canadians at a crucial period of our history.

POSTSCRIPT

As indicated in the preface, this is an incomplete manuscript.

Cheryl had much more material and hoped to trace some of the seamen and how their lives went on after their sojourn in Canada.

Sadly, with her premature demise, this is not to be.

What we do know is that after leaving Canadian waters the gunboats spent time in Nova Scotia, then headed to the Caribbean. By early 1870, they were all back in Portsmouth Harbour, England, where the crew would have either been assigned to other naval vessels, or been paid off and sent home.

Some details are known of the three main officers.

Lt. Spencer R. Huntley died aboard the *Cherub* sometime between late 1868 and early 1869 of illness.

Henry Stephenson, who was the son of the eleventh Duke of Norfolk, went on to marry the daughter of the seventeenth Lord Saltoun. He was a close friend of Edward VII and was one of only fifty people allowed to view that sovereign's body after his death. Stephenson died in 1919 and is buried in Hanwell, England.

After his time in Canadian waters, Alington went on to serve in Africa and the Mediterranean. In 1899, he inherited the family home Swinhope Hall and thereafter lived the life of a country gentleman. He died December 7, 1925.

I had the privilege of meeting Alington's granddaughter,

Mrs. Jean Howard, about nine years ago and she treated me to a delightful lunch at her home in Knightsbridge. She did not have a lot of details about Alington's later career, but did tell me that the family thought of his naval days with a certain sense of amusement. There seems to be a suspicion that he had "ladies" whom he left behind in each port. She had fond memories of him as a loving, warm grandfather.

Mrs. Howard herself had made a contribution to history as one of the young women who were part of the Enigma project during World War II. At the time of our meeting she was still largely bound by the Official Secrets Act, but she was able to share a few vignettes.

But, alas, that is another story.

Sandra MacDonald
London, England
May 2017

ACKNOWLEDGEMENTS

A number of people have provided invaluable assistance in preparing this book. First and foremost, thanks go to my sister, Sandra MacDonald, who has provided encouragement, emotional and financial support, and research assistance. Thanks also to the members of the Dunnville District Heritage Association, especially Estelle Pringle, founding member and past president; the late Stan Parker and Debbie Parker; and April Cormaci, current president. I first became aware of the *Britomart* when working on DDHA's community history and quickly became fascinated. The late Merle Knight, curator at Haldimand County Museum, provided some early leads as did John Burtniak, former special collections librarian at Brock University. Bill Yeager, curator at Eva Brook Donly Museum (Norfolk Heritage Centre) first drew my attention to Alexander McNeilledge's diary and the Port Dover *New Dominion*, both of which have proved very useful. Numerous other individuals have encouraged me with their kind words and interest, including Ian Bell, former curator at Port Dover Harbour Museum, Fred Briggs and the staff at Huron County Museum and Archives, Goderich. Emotional support has also come from my family — my daughter Catherine Riley-Arenberg and my husband Dan Riley.

Cheryl MacDonald

Fall 2016

ENDNOTES

PROLOGUE

1. Cheryl MacDonald (ed.), *Grand Heritage: A History of Dunnville and the Townships of Canborough, Dunn, Moulton, Sherbrooke and South Cayuga* (Dunnville, ON: Dunnville District Heritage Association, 1992), 330.

2. *Grand River Sachem*, November 1866. Dunnville had its own newspaper at the time, the *Luminary*, but no issues have survived.

3. Ibid.

CHAPTER 1

1. *Hamilton Evening Times*, January 31, 1866.

2. *Hamilton Evening Times*, November 29, 1865.

3. Lady Monck's diary, June 22, 1867, quoted in David A. Wilson, *Thomas D'Arcy McGee*, vol. 2: *The Extreme Moderate, 1857–1868* (Montreal: McGill-Queen's University Press, 2013).

4. *Hamilton Evening Times*, October 26, 1865.

5. (Montreal: John Lovell, 1904) p. 17–18, quoted in DA.

6. Wilson, *Thomas D'Arcy McGee*, Vol. 2, 105–6.

7. Ibid., 229.

8. Michael Murphy, quoted in Wilson, *Thomas D'Arcy McGee*, vol. 2, 152–53.

9. Wilson, *Thomas D'Arcy McGee*, Vol. 2, 266.

10. *Orangeville Sun*, quoted in *Hamilton Evening Times*, December 19, 1864.

11. Ibid.

12. *Hamilton Evening Times*, December 15, 1865.

13. *Hamilton Evening Times*, October 23, 1865.

14. *Hamilton Evening Times*, March 9, 1866.

15. *Hamilton Evening Times*, March 10, 1866.

CHAPTER 2

1. George Wells, "The Fenian Raid in Willoughby," in *Welland County Historical Society Papers and Records*, Vol. II (Welland, ON: Welland Tribune and Telegraph Limited, 1926), 58.

2. E.A. Cruikshank, quoted in "Sam Johnston, Smuggler, Soldier and

Bearer of News," by Louis Blake Duff, in *Welland County Historical Society Papers and Records*, Vol. II (Welland, ON: Welland Tribune and Telegraph Limited, 1926), 91–92.

3. Ibid., 92.

4. Ibid., 75.

5. G.F.G. Stanley, *Canada's Soldiers* (Toronto: Macmillan Canada, 1960), 228.

6. *Hamilton Evening Times*, October 12, 1865.

7. *Hamilton Evening Times*, June 6, 1866.

8. Cruikshank, in *Welland County Historical Society Papers*, Vol. II, 33.

9. *Globe*, June 1, 3, 5, quoted in Wilson, *Thomas D'Arcy McGee*, vol. 2.

10. Robert Larmour, "With Booker's Column: Personal Reminiscences of the Events of the Fenian Raid of June, 1866," *Canadian Magazine* 10. See also Peter Vronsky, *Ridgeway: The American Fenian Invasion and the 1866 Battle that Made Canada* (Toronto: Allen Lane, 2011).

11. Denison, George T. *Soldiering in Canada; Recollections and Experiences.* Toronto: George Morang and Company, 1900.

12. *Hamilton Evening Times*, September 11, 1866.

13. *Hamilton Evening Times*, July 4, 1866.

14. *Hamilton Evening Times*, September 11, 1866.

15. Denison, George T. *Soldiering in Canada; Recollections and Experiences.* (Toronto: George Morang and Company, 1900), 123.

16. *Hamilton Evening Times*, August 30, 1866

17. *Hamilton Evening Times*, August 15, 1866.

18. *Hamilton Evening Times*, August 17, 1866.

19. *Hamilton Evening Times*, July 20, 1866.

20. Menlo Hoover diary.

CHAPTER 3

1. "Speech on Motion for an Address to Her Majesty in Favour of Confederation," quoted in Wilson, *Thomas D'Arcy McGee*, Vol. II, 211.

2. Bernard Bailyn, Robert Dallek, David Davis, David Donald and John Thomas, *The Great Republic: A History of the American People*, 2nd ed. (Lexington, VA: D.C. Heath and Company, 1981), 499.

3. *Janesville Gazette*, December 15, 1864.

4. "Rush-Bagot Treaty," Wikisource.org, accessed May 4, 2017, https://en.wikisource.org/wiki/Rush-Bagot_Treaty.

5.   The *St. Catharines Constitutional*, April 9, 1868, tells a different story: "The American government during the war gave notice, as we all remember, to the British government of the discontinuance of the convention which prohibited either nation from putting gunboats on the lakes. They soon after put a number of them there . . ." The article goes on to say that because the American gunboats were "found to be very expensive and very useless, the House of Representatives has stricken out from the appropriation bill the item which provided for the maintenance of these vessels. The gunboats will, therefore, be discontinued unless the Senate shall refuse, which is not likely, to concur in the decision of the other House."

6.   H.A. Washington, ed., *The Writings of Thomas Jefferson* (Cambridge: Cambridge University Press), 75–76.

7.   Adams, quoted in Walter A. McDougall, *Promised Land, Crusader State: The American Encounter with the World since 1776* (Boston: Houghton Mifflin, 1997), 78.

8.   Wilson, *Thomas D'Arcy McGee*, Vol. 2.

9.   Michel to Governor-General Monck, March 14, 1866, Canadian Ministry of Marine files, RG 9, Series IC8, Vol. 8.

10. Michel to Secretary of State for War, June 4, 1866, Colonial Office 1866 ADM 1/5997.

11. *New York Herald*, reprinted in *Hamilton Evening Times*, May 27, 1867.

12. Seneca Centennial Historical Committee, *The Township of Seneca History: Centennial Year 1867–1967* (Seneca, ON: Seneca Centennial Historical Committee).

13. *London Free Press*, June 8 and 9, 1866.

14. *Grand River Sachem*, July 25, 1866.

CHAPTER 4

1.   McCallum to Macdonald, April 6, 1865.

2.   Ibid.

3.   Ibid.

4.   William Johnston, William G.P. Rawling, Richard H. Gimblett and John MacFarlane, *The Seabound Coast: The Official History of the Royal Canadian Navy, 1867–1939*, Vol. 1. (Toronto: Dundurn Press, 2011), 4.

5.   Ibid.

6.   Monck to James Hope, March 9, 1866.

7.   The report actually says "T.H. Bobb," but gives the owner as L.

McCallum; there is no doubt that this was the *W.T. Robb*. The issue of who paid for what caused some occasional confusion, but on July 26, 1866, De Horsey reiterated his understanding of the situation in a letter to Governor-General Monck: "I have the honour to inform your Excellency that I understood Vice Admiral Sir James Hope to have agreed on the part of the Admiralty to bear all expenses connected with working the Gunboats (including therefore their fuel) except their hire and equipment"; however, he offered to verify this understanding. On August 9, he confirmed the arrangement in another letter to Monck: "I have the honor to inform Your Excellency that I am instructed by Vice Admiral Sir J. Hope that he agrees on the part of the Admiralty to bear all expenses connected with the working of those Gunboats (including therefore the fuel) except their hire and equipment." Canadian Ministry of Marine files, RG 9 Series IC8, Vol. 8.

8. Canada, Sessional Paper (1867-8) No. 37. Information respecting Government Gunboats, for the years 1866 and 1867.

9. Ibid.

10. *Canadian News*, August 30, 1866, 137.

11. Algernon De Horsey, "Letter of Proceedings," June 7, 1866, Admiralty and Ministry of Defence, ADM 128/24.

12. Untitled document, August 15, 1866, which presumably accompanied the bill of sale for the *Rescue*. Canadian Ministry of Marine files, RG9 Series IC8, Vol. 8.

13. Wyatt to Napier, June 28, 1866, Canadian Ministry of Marine files, RG 9 Series IC8, Vol. 8.

14. John A. McDonald, *Troublous Times in Canada*, (Toronto: W.S. Johnstone, 1910), 102.

15. Canadian Ministry of Marine files, RG 9 Series IC8, Vol. 8.

16. Richard J. Wright, "Green Flags and Red-Coated Gunboats: Naval Activities on the Great Lakes During the Fenian Scares, 1866–1870," *Inland Seas* 22 (Summer 1966), 97; De Horsey, "Letter of Proceedings."

17. Wyatt, "Calendar," Canadian Ministry of Marine files, RG 9 Series IC8, Vol. 8.

18. *Robertson's Landmarks of Toronto: A Collection of Historical Sketches of the Old Town of York from 1792 until 1833, and of Toronto from 1834 to 1898* (Toronto: J. Ross Robertson, 1898), accessed May 1, 2017, https://archive.org/details/landmarkstoronto03robeuoft.

19. Canadian Ministry of Marine files, 1866, RG 9 Series IC8, Vol. 9.

20. Leasing agreement for *Royal*, June 4, 1866, Canadian Ministry of

Marine files, RG 9 Series IC8, Vol. 9.

21. Letter from McCallum, June 25,1866, Canadian Ministry of Marine files, RG Series IC8, Vol. 9.

22. McCallum to Wyatt, August 30, 1866, Canadian Ministry of Marine files, RG 9 Series IC8, Vol. 9.

23. Letter from McDougall, September 15, 1866, Canadian Ministry of Marine files, RG 9 Series IC8, Vol. 9.

24. S. Morrison to McDougall, July 6, 1866, Canadian Ministry of Marine files, RG 9 Series IC8, Vol. 8.

25. Letter to Wyatt from Acting Minister of Marine, July 6, 1866, Canadian Ministry of Marine files, RG 9 Series IC8, Vol. 8. It is possible that the author of the letter is McDougall, but the name has been scratched out.

26. McMicken, memo, June 28, 1866.

27. Canada, Sessional Paper (1867-8) No. 37. Information respecting Government Gunboats, for the years 1866 and 1867.

28. Hood to Major General James Lindsay, Montreal, June 27, 1866, Canadian Ministry of Marine files, RG 9 Series IC8.

29. De Horsey to Monck, June 30, 1866, Canadian Ministry of Marine files, RG 9 Series IC8, Vol. 8.

30. Monck to Cardwell from Ottawa, June 14, 1866.

31. Cardwell to Monck, June 30.

32. De Horsey to Monck, June 30, 1866, Canadian Ministry of Marine files, RG 9 Series IC8, Vol. 8.

33. Ibid.

34. Ibid.

35. Fairlie to Wyatt, June 28, 1866, Canadian Ministry of Marine files, RG 9 Series IC8, Vol. 8.

36. Wyatt to McDougall, July 12, 1866, Canadian Ministry of Marine files, RG 9 Series IC8, Vol. 8.

37. Report from Wyatt, July 5, 1866, Canadian Ministry of Marine files, RG 9 Series IC8, Vol. 8.

38. Ibid.

39. Ibid.

40. McDougall to Monck, July 5, 1866, Canadian Ministry of Marine files, RG 9 Series IC8, Vol. 8.

41. Pridgeon to Wyatt, July 9, 1866, Canadian Ministry of Marine files, RG 9 Series IC8, Vol. 8.

42. Cook Brothers to Wyatt, July 9, 1866, Canadian Ministry of Marine files, RG 9 Series IC8, Vol. 8.

43. Wyatt to McDougall, July 9, 1866, Canadian Ministry of Marine files, RG 9 Series IC8, Vol. 8.

44. Wyatt to McDougall, July 13, 1866, Canadian Ministry of Marine files, RG 9 Series IC8, Vol. 8.

45. Risely to Vansittart, July 23, 1866, Canadian Ministry of Marine files, RG 9 Series IC8, Vol 8.

46. McDougall to Wyatt, July 27, 1866, Canadian Ministry of Marine files, RG 9 Series IC8 Vol 8.

47. Undated letter from Risley to McDougall; written before August 10 as that date is referred to.

48. Undated letter from Risley to McDougall.

49. Wyatt to Gehartys, June 4, 1867, Canadian Ministry of Marine files, RG 9, Series IC8, Vol 9.

50. Wright, "Green Flags."

51. July 16, 1866, Canadian Ministry of Marine files, RG 9 Series IC8, Vol. 8.

52. Alexander Cameron to McDougall, July 21, 1866, Canadian Ministry of Marine files, RG 9 Series IC8, Vol. 8.

53. Letter from Walter McCrea and Archibald Allan, July 27, 1866, Canadian Ministry of Marine files, RG 9 Series IC8, Vol. 8.

54. McDougall, July 28, 1866, Canadian Ministry of Marine files, RG 9 Series IC8, Vol. 8.

55. McDougall to Cameron, August 13, 1866, Canadian Ministry of Marine files, RG 9 Series IC8, Vol. 8.

56. Wyatt to McDougall, July 24, 1866, Canadian Ministry of Marine files, RG 9 Series IC8, Vol. 8.

57. Ibid.

58. Wyatt to McDougall, July 28, 1866, Canadian Ministry of Marine files, RG 9 Series IC8, Vol. 8.

59. Rice to Wyatt, October 6, 1866, Canadian Ministry of Marine files, RG 9 Series IC8, Vol. 9.

60. Heron to Wyatt, October 10, 1866, Canadian Ministry of Marine files, RG 9 Series IC8, Vol. 9.

61. Gibbon to Lieutenant-Colonel Earle, Montreal, June 18, 1866.

CHAPTER 5

1. Michael Lewis, *The Navy in Transition* (London: Hodder and Stoughton,

1965), 12.

2.   Ibid, 13.

3.   Michael Lewis, *British Ships and Seamen* (London: Longmans, Green & Co., 1940), 50.

4.   Depending on the source, Britomart was either a legendary Welsh princess or an ancient Cretan goddess who was the patron of fishermen and hunters. A number of British vessels bore the same name both before and after the gunboat under discussion.

5.   Wright, "Green Flags," 100–101. The *Britomart* was launched May 1860. *Heron* was two inches shorter, but otherwise identical, while the *Cherub* was just an inch shorter and eight inches wider. *Cherub* was the newest of the three gunboats sent to Canada.

6.   *Britomart* log, ADM 53/9542.

7.   *Cherub* log, ADM 53/9566.

8.   *Britomart* log, August 3, 1866, ADM 53/9542.

9.   *British Daily Whig*, July 18, 1866. The newspaper also gave the name of the *Britomart* commander as Atington, rather than Alington, and provided no first name for Stephenson, commander of the *Heron*.

10. *British Daily Whig*, July 21, 1866.

11. *British Daily Whig*, July 26, 1866.

12. *Halifax Citizen*, August 7, 1866.

13. *London Free Press*, August 17, 1866.

14. *British Daily Whig*, August 17, 1866. The *Britomart*, still disabled from the accident in the Lachine Canal, arrived August 6 according to the log, ADM 53/9468.

15. *British Daily Whig*, August 10, 1866. *Britomart* left for Port Dalhousie on August 9 and remained there until August 21. *Britomart* log, ADM 53/9468.

16. *British Daily Whig*, August 11, 1866.

17. *Daily News* [Kingston], August 10, 1866. The *Britomart* and *Cherub* had already left Kingston by this time.

18. *Daily News* [Kingston], August 11, 1866.

19. *Daily News* [Kingston], August 13, 1866.

20. *Grand River Sachem*, August 15, 1866; reprint of Kingston newspaper report.

21. *St. Catharines Constitutional*, August16, 1866.

22. *Hamilton Evening Times*, August 16, 1866.

23. *London Free Press*, August 18, 1866.

24. Historical Firearms, "Ordnance of the Week: The Armstrong Gun," n.d., accessed May 4, 2017, http://www.historicalfirearms.info/post/43264118681/ordnance-of-the-week-the-armstrong-gun-in-1854.

25. Victorian Forts and Artillery, "Armstrong: The Great Gunmaker," n.d., accessed May 4, 2017, http://www.victorianforts.co.uk/armstrong.htm.

26. *Grand River Sachem*, August 28, 1867.

27. *St. Catharines Constitutional*, August 16, 1866, 2.

28. *London Free Press*, August 22, 1866.

29. *Hamilton Spectator*, August 20, 1866.

30. Ibid.

31. Ibid.

32. Ibid.

33. *Daily Leader* [Toronto], September 19, 1866.

34. Dunnville *Independent*, reprinted in *Grand River Sachem*, September 19, 1866.

CHAPTER 6

1. *Daily News* [Kingston], August 13, 1866.

2. Ibid.

3. *Owen Sound Comet*, September 7, 1866.

4. *St. Catharines Constitutional*, August 16, 1866, 2.

5. *Daily Leader* [Toronto], August 20, 1866.

6. *Evening Journal* [St. Catharines], August 21, 1866, 4.

7. Dr. John Weaver pointed out the *Oxford English Dictionary* meaning: "b. euphem. Exhilarated with drink, slightly intoxicated," which was still in use until 1884. In *English through the Ages*, William Brohaugh states "jolly" meant "lustful" from around 1450 to 1600 (p. 37).

8. Lewis, *The Navy in Transition*, 168.

9. Ibid., 217.

10. Ibid., 214.

11. Ibid., 188.

12. Ibid.

13. Ibid., 168. According to Lewis, men who were shanghaied by press gangs often had their street clothes burned and so had no choice but to wear the slops.

14. Ibid., 225–26.

15. Ibid., 267.

16. Ibid., 270.

17. This number excludes officers. The men in the survey did not necessarily serve at the same time: Some left the navy when their term of duty was up; others were transferred to different vessels or died.

18. Ages were calculated as of August 1, 1866, based on dates of birth given in personnel records.

19. Jon Henley, "The Rise and Rise of the Tattoo," *The Guardian*, July 20, 2010, accessed November 15, 2015, https://www.theguardian.com/artanddesign/2010/jul/20/tattoos.

20. *Britomart* log, April 20, 1868.

21. Dunnville *Luminary*, quoted in MacDonald (ed.), *Grand Heritage*, 151–52. The article in the *Luminary* was likely reprinted from the *St. Catharines Constitutional*.

22. Without extensive information, it is difficult to determine whether the attendance at Dean's funeral, and presumably at those of other sailors, was motivated by patriotic sentiments or by the Victorian fascination with funerary ritual. Undoubtedly a certain number of those attending the funerals did so out of curiosity and because of the entertainment value entailed in the pageantry of a military ceremony.

23. Boredom was a problem on many navy vessels, as H.W.F. Baynham observes (345). "A Seaman in H.M.S. *Leander*, 1863–66," *Mariner's Mirror* (1965): 343–53.

24. Lewis, *The Navy in Transition*, 253.

25. Ibid., 256.

26. *Britomart* log, September 27, 1866.

27. Meanwhile, a number of larger vessels remained in Halifax harbour. This apparently had not been done before and caused some difficulties. HMS *Aurora* was damaged by ice moved about by rising tides, prompting De Horsey to draw up extensive instructions on preparing naval vessels for wintering in Canada. De Horsey, "Letter of Proceedings."

28. *Globe*, quoted in *Goderich Signal*, November 8, 1866.

29. *Daily News* [Kingston], November 27, 1866; *Daily Leader* [Toronto], March 30, 1867; *Daily Leader* [Toronto], April 2, 1868; *Goderich Signal*, February 28, 1867.

30. *Montreal Herald* and *Daily Commercial Gazette*, December 12, 1866.

31. *London Free Press*, quoted in the *Norfolk Reformer*, May 16, 1867.

32. *Daily News* [Kingston], September 4, 1868. Lady Jane VanKoughnet, *The Von Gochnats* (privately printed, 1910), 13–16.

33. *Daily Leader* [Toronto], November 29, 1866.

34. *Daily News* [Kingston], October 10, 1866.

35. *Goderich Signal*, January 3, 1867.

36. *Grand River Sachem*, February 13, 1867.

37. *Hamilton Evening Times*, March 29, 1867.

CHAPTER 7

1. Eugene L. Rasor, *Reform in the Royal Navy: A Social History of the Lower Deck 1859 to 1880* (Hamden, CT: Archon Books, 1976), 39.

2. Ibid., 15.

3. Ibid., 44.

4. N.A.M. Rodger, Articles of War. Hampshire: Kenneth Mason, 1982, 13.

5. Ibid., 46.

6. Lewis, *The Navy in Transition*, 169n2.

7. "Return of Convictions — Haldimand and Norfolk," various newspaper reports.

8. Ibid.

9. *Cherub* log, October 10, 1866, and January 5, 1867, ADM 53/9566.

10. *Cherub* log, September 1, 1868, ADM 53/9567.

11. *Cherub* log, January 5, 1867, ADM 53/9566.

12. Ibid.

13. *Cherub* log, September 10, 1866, and September 28–30, 1866, ADM 53/9566.

14. *Cherub* log, October 26, 1866, ADM 53/9566.

15. Correspondence with Dan McPherson, Museum Assistant, Huron Historic Gaol, August 20, 2005.

16. Vice-Admiral Colomb, quoted in Lewis, *The Navy in Transition*, 168.

17. Baynham, "A Seaman in *HMS Leander*," 350.

18. Lewis, *The Navy in Transition*, 169n2.

19. *Britomart* log, August 10, 1866, ADM 53/9542. This was the first punishment warrant issued; Lloyd received thirty-six lashes.

20. *Cherub* log, April 25, 1868, ADM 53/9567. This was the most serious summary punishment available. Unfortunately, a search at the British National Archives, Kew, has failed to turn up any warrants; one librarian suggested these records may not have been preserved by the admiralty.

21. *Cherub* log, February 18, 1867, ADM 53/9566.

22. The *Cherub* had been ordered to Lake Ontario on May 28, 1868, according to the *Goderich Star*, June 5, 1868.

23. *Hamilton Evening Times*, June 19, 1868.

24. Rasor, *Reform in the Royal Navy*, 17–18.

25. *Britomart* log, September 16, 20, 28, 30, 1866, ADM 53/9542.

26. *Cherub* log, January 3 and 5, 1867, ADM 53/9566.

27. *Cherub* log, April 3 and 4, 1867, ADM 53/9566.

28. *Britomart* log, October 17 and 18, 1867, ADM 53/9543.

29. *Britomart* log, March 15 and 16, 1868, ADM 53/9543.

30. Diary of Alexander McNeilledge, July 24, 1867, Norfolk Historical Society, Eva Brook Donly Museum, Simcoe, Ontario.

31. For a discussion of the impact of leave on discipline problems, see Rasor, *Reform in the Royal Navy*, 17.

32. Lewis discusses some of these aspects in *The Navy in Transition*, 172–73.

33. De Horsey, "Letter of Proceedings."

34. De Horsey, "Precautions Against Desertion," April 15, 1867, ADM 128/25.

35. Judith Fingard, *Jack in Port* (Toronto: University of Toronto Press, 1982), 29.

36. Telegram from Cochrane to Hope, May 9, 1867, ADM 128/25.

37. Hope to Cochrane, May 10, 1867, ADM 128/25.

38. De Horsey, Memorandum, April 15, 1867, ADM 128/25.

39. Ibid.

40. *Goderich Signal*, January 3, 1867.

41. Extract of memorandum from Hope to De Horsey, February 23, 1867, ADM 128/5.

42. De Horsey, Memorandum.

43. *Daily Leader* [Toronto], October 11 and 12, 1866.

44. *Cherub* log, October 27, 1866, and November 14, 1866, ADM 53/9566.

45. *Britomart* log, January 1867, ADM 53/9542.

46. *Prescott Telegraph*, quoted in *Hamilton Evening Times*, May 29, 1867.

47. De Horsey, Memorandum.

48. *Daily Leader* [Toronto], February 8, 1867.

49. *Globe*, June 24, 1867.

50. Among the letters is one from De Horsey dated May 8, 1867, ADM 128/25.

51. *Hamilton Evening Times*, April 3, 1867, and *Daily Leader* [Toronto], April 4, 1867.

52. *Daily Leader* [Toronto], April 4, 1867.

53. *Goderich Signal*, November 29, 1866.

EPILOGUE

1. *Daily Leader* [Toronto], June 10, 1868.

2. *Hamilton Evening Times*, June 9, 1868.

3. *Daily Leader* [Toronto], June 10, 1868.

4. *Hamilton Evening Times*, May 29, 1868.

5. Dunnville *Luminary*, quoted in *New Dominion*, June 5, 1868.

6. *Goderich Star*, June 5, 1868.

7. *Buffalo Commercial Advertiser*, July 14, 1868.

8. *Detroit Post*, quoted in the *Daily Leader* [Toronto], August 21, 1868.

9. Michel to Monck, March 28, 1867, ADM 1/6026.

10. *St. Catharines Constitutional*, April 9, 1868.

11. *Hamilton Evening Times*, October 2, 1868.

12. *Hamilton Evening Times*, October 24, 1868.

13. *St. Catharines Constitutional*, October 29, 1868.

14. *New Dominion*, October 30, 1868.

15. *Britomart* and *Cherub* spent some time protecting the Atlantic fisheries against American poachers. The *Britomart* was sold in 1892, becoming a mooring hulk, and was broken up in 1946. *Cherub* was sold and broken up in Jamaica in June 1897. Antony Preston and John Major, *Send a Gunboat: The Victorian Navy and Supremacy at Sea, 1854–1904* (London: Longmans, Green & Co., 1967), 206; Wright, "Green Flags," 103.

16. *New Dominion*, October 30, 1868.

17. *Canadian News*, November 19, 1868.

BIBLIOGRAPHY

BOOKS

Bailyn, Bernard, Robert Dallek, David Davis, David Donald and John Thomas. *The Great Republic: A History of the American People*, 2nd ed. Lexington, VA: D.C. Heath and Company, 1981.

Beers, J.H. & Co. *History of the Great Lakes*. Cleveland, OH: Freshwater Press Inc., 1972. Originally published 1899.

Bramford, Don. *Freshwater Heritage: A History of Sail on the Great Lakes, 1670–1918*. Toronto: Natural Heritage Books, 2007.

Brohaugh, William. *English Through the Ages*. Cincinnati, OH: Writer's Digest Books, 1998.

Burke, Bernard, and Ashworth P. Burke. *A Genealogical and Heraldic History of the Peerage and Baronetage, the Privy Council, Knightage and Companionage*. London: Harrison & Sons, 1908.

Canadian Encyclopedia. Toronto: McLelland and Stewart, 1999.

Denison, George T. *Soldiering in Canada; Recollections and Experiences*. Toronto: George Morang and Company, 1900.

Docker, John Thornley. *Dunnville Heroes: The W.T. Robb and the Dunnville Naval Brigade in the 1866 Fenian Invasion*. Dunnville, ON: Dunnville District Heritage Association, 2003.

Duff, Louis Blake. "Sam Johnston, Smuggler, Soldier and Bearer of News." in *Welland County Historical Society Papers and Records*, Vol. II. Welland, ON: Welland Tribune and Telegraph Limited, 1926.

Fingard, Judith. *Jack in Port*. Toronto: University of Toronto Press, 1982.

Holland, J. Rose, et al. "Imperial Defence 1815–1870," in *The Cambridge History of the British Empire*, Vol. II: *The Growth of the New Empire, 1783–1870*, 806–41. Cambridge: Cambridge University Press, 1940.

Johnston, William, William G.P. Rawling, Richard H. Gimblett and

John MacFarlane. *The Seabound Coast: The Official History of the Royal Canadian Navy, 1867–1939*, Vol. I. Toronto: Dundurn Press, 2011.

LeCaron, Henri. *Twenty-Five Years in the Secret Service: The Recollections of a Spy*. London: W. Heinemann, 1892.

Lewis, Michael. *British Ships and British Seamen*. London: Longmans, Green & Co., 1940.

———. *The Navy in Transition: A Social History 1814–1864*. London: Hodder and Stoughton, 1965.

MacDonald, Cheryl, ed. *Grand Heritage: A History of Dunnville and the Townships of Canborough, Dunn, Moulton, Sherbrooke and South Cayuga*. Dunnville, ON: Dunnville District Heritage Association, 1992.

McDonald, John A. *Troublous Times in Canada*. Toronto: W.S. Johnstone, 1910.

McDougall, Walter A. *Promised Land, Crusader State: The American Encounter with the World Since 1776*. Boston: Houghton Mifflin, 1997.

Oxford English Dictionary. "Jolly." Oxford: Oxford University Press, 1989.

Pappalardo, Bruno. *Royal Naval Lieutenants' Passing Certificates 1691–1901*, Vols. 289 and 290. Kew: List and Index Society, Public Record Office, 2001.

Preston, Antony, and John Major. *Send a Gunboat: The Victorian Navy and Supremacy at Sea, 1854–1904*. London: Longmans, Green & Co., 1967.

Rasor, Eugene L. *Reform in the Royal Navy: A Social History of the Lower Deck 1859 to 1880*. Hamden, CT: Archon Books, 1976.

Robertson's Landmarks of Toronto: A Collection of Historical Sketches of the Old Town of York from 1792 until 1833, and of Toronto from 1834 to 1898. Toronto: J. Ross Robertson, 1898. Accessed May 1, 2017. https://archive.org/details/landmarkstoronto03robeuoft.

Rodger, N.A.M. *The Articles of War*. Hampshire: Kenneth Mason Publications Ltd., 1982.

———. *The Command of the Ocean: A Naval History of Britain, 1649–1815*. New York: W.W. Norton, 2005.

———. *The Safeguard of the Sea: A Naval History of Britain 660–1649*. London: W.W. Norton, 1997.

Seneca Centennial Historical Committee. *The Township of Seneca History: Centennial Year 1867–1967*. Seneca, ON: Seneca Centennial Historical Committee.

Senior, Hereward. *The Fenians and Canada*. Toronto: Macmillan Canada, 1978.

———. *The Last Invasion of Canada: The Fenian Raids 1866–1870*. Toronto: Dundurn Press, in collaboration with Canadian War Museum and Canadian Museum of Civilization, 1991.

Stanley, G.F.G. *Canada's Soldiers*. Toronto: Macmillan Canada, 1960.

Stephenson, John, ed. *A Royal Correspondence: Letters of King Edward VII and King George V to Admiral Sir Henry F. Stephenson*. London: Macmillan, 1938.

VanKoughnet, Lady Jane. *The Von Gochnats*. Privately printed, 1910.

Vronsky, Peter. *Ridgeway: The American Fenian Invasion and the 1866 Battle that Made Canada*. Toronto: Allen Lane, 2011.

Washington, H.A., ed. *The Writings of Thomas Jefferson*. Cambridge: Cambridge University Press.

Wells, George. "The Fenian Raid in Willoughby." in *Welland County Historical Society Papers and Records*, Vol. II. Welland, ON: Welland Tribune and Telegraph Limited, 1926.

Wilson, David A. *Thomas D'Arcy McGee*, Vol. 2: *The Extreme Moderate, 1857–1868*. Montreal: McGill-Queen's University Press, 2013.

ARTICLES

Barry, James P. "U.S. Canada Border Frictions: The Great Lakes–St. Lawrence Border, Parts IV and V." *Inland Seas* 45, no. 4 (1989): 256–71.

Bauer, K. Jack. "List of United States Warships on the Great Lakes,

1796–1941." *Ontario History* 56 (1964): 58–64.

Baxter, Colin F. "The Duke Somerset and the Creation of the British Ironclad Navy, 1859–1866." *Mariner's Mirror* 63, no. 3 (1979): 279–84.

Baynham, H.W.F. "A Seaman in H.M.S. *Leander*, 1863–66." *Mariner's Mirror* (1965): 343–53.

Historical Firearms. "Ordnance of the Week: The Armstrong Gun." n.d, Accessed May 4, 2017. http://www.historicalfirearms.info/post/43264118681/ordnance-of-the-week-the-armstrong-gun-in-1854.

Landon, Fred. "Gunboats on the Lower Great Lakes During the Fenian Scare." *Inland Seas* 19 (Spring 1963): 47–54.

Larmour, Robert. "With Booker's Column: Personal Reminiscences of the Events of the Fenian Raid of June, 1866." *Canadian Magazine* 10, no. 2 (1897): 121–27; no. 3 (1898): 228–31.

Macpherson, K.R. "Lists of Vessels Employed on British Naval Service on the Great Lakes, 1755–1875." *Ontario History* 55 (1963): 173–78.

Neidhardt, W.S. "The American Government and the Fenian Brotherhood: A Study in Mutual Political Opportunism." *Ontario History* 64 (1972): 27–44.

———. "The Fenian Brotherhood and Western Ontario: The Final Years." *Ontario History* 60 (1968): 149–61.

Peters, Scott M. "Military Vessels on the Great Lakes." *Michigan Archaeologist* 37, no. 1: 25–33.

Robb, Andrew. "The Toronto Globe and the Defence of Canada, 1861–1866." *Ontario History* 64 (1972): 65–77.

Ruddy, Michael. "Here Comes that Damned Green Flag Again: The Fenians and the American Civil War." *Civil War Times*, April 2003. http://freepages.genealogy.rootsweb.ancestry.com/~mruddy/GreeenFlag1.htm.

Senior, Hereward. "Quebec and the Fenians." *Canadian Historical Review* 48, no. 1 (March 1967): 26–44.

Stouffer, Allen, P. "Canadian American Relations in the Shadow of the

Civil War." *Dalhousie Review* 57, no.1 (1977): 332–46.

Victorian Forts and Artillery. "Armstrong: The Great Gunmaker." n.d. Accessed May 4, 2017. http://www.victorianforts.co.uk/armstrong.htm.

Wright, Richard J. "Green Flags and Red-Coated Gunboats: Naval Activities on the Great Lakes During the Fenian Scares, 1866–1870." *Inland Seas* 22 (Summer 1966): 92–110.

NEWSPAPERS
British Daily Whig (Kingston)

Buffalo Commercial Advertiser

Canadian News

Daily Leader (Toronto)

Daily News (Kingston)

Evening Journal (St. Catharines)

Globe (Toronto)

Goderich Signal

Goderich Star

Grand River Sachem (Caledonia)

Halifax Citizen

Hamilton Evening Times

Hamilton Spectator

Janesville Gazette

London Free Press

Montreal Herald and Daily Commercial Gazette

New Dominion (Port Dover)

Norfolk Reformer (Simcoe)

Ottawa Times

Owen Sound Comet

Owen Sound Advertiser

Port Dover Maple Leaf

St. Catharines Constitutional

Simcoe Reformer

The Times (England)

Tillsonberg Observer

ONLINE SOURCES

Government of Canada. *Canadian Military Heritage*.

The Mudcat Café. "Jolly Jack Tar."

"Rush-Bagot Treaty." Wikisource.org. Accessed May 4, 2017. https://en.wikisource.org/wiki/Rush-Bagot_Treaty.

GOVERNMENT DOCUMENTS

Library and Archives Canada

Canada, Sessional Paper (1867-8) No. 37. Information respecting Government Gunboats, for the years 1866 and 1867.

Canadian Ministry of Marine files

RG 9, Series IC8, Vol. 8, "Gunboats" file Nos. 1–20, 1866.

RG 9, Series IC8, Vol. 8, "Gunboats" files Nos. 21–6, 1866.

RG 9, Series IC8, Vol. 9, "Gunboats" files Nos. 63–109, 1866.

RG 9, Series IC8, Vol. 9 "Gunboats" file Nos. 113–63, 1867–1868.

National Archives of the United Kingdom, Kew, England

Admiralty Papers: Records of the Navy Board and the Board of Admiralty.

Admiralty and Ministry of Defence, Navy Department: Correspondence and Papers, In-letters and papers: 1860–1869

Colonial Office 1866, ADM 1/5977.

Colonial Office 1867, ADM 1/6026.

Colonial Office 1868, ADM 1/6071.

The protection of the Canadian frontier against Fenians, January 5, 1866 to January 12, 1867; ADM 128/24; August 12, 1866, to May 31, 1968, ADM 128/25.

Records of Service, ADM 139.

Admiralty: Royal Marines: Attestation Forms, Plymouth Division—Attestations and Discharges 1805–1883, ADM 157.

Admiralty Officers Service Records (Series III) 1756–1966, ADM 196/24/151.

Admiralty and Ministry of Defence, Navy Department: Ships Logs

ADM 53/9468, HMG *Heron*, April 3, 1866–April 19, 1867.

ADM 53/9469, HMG *Heron*, April 20, 1867–July 4, 1868.

ADM 53/9475, HMG *Heron*, July 5, 1868–September 4, 1869.

ADM 53/9542, HMG *Britomart*, March 31, 1866–September 5, 1867.

ADM 53/9543, HMG *Britomart*, September 6, 1867–January 18, 1869.

ADM 53/9566, HMG *Cherub*, April 18, 1866–November 1, 1867.

ADM 53/9567, HMG *Cherub*, November 2, 1867–May 12, 1869.

UNPUBLISHED SOURCES

Diary of Alexander McNeilledge. Norfolk Historical Society, Eva Brook Donly Museum, Simcoe, Ontario.

Sandra MacDonald, discussions with Jan Alington Howard (b. August 23, 1917) London, England, 2004.

INDEX